LEGACY OF DEATH

LEGACY OF

BARBARA LEVY

DEATH

PRENTICE-HALL, INC. ❧ *Englewood Cliffs, N. J.*

Library of Congress Cataloging in Publication Data
Levy, Barbara.
  Legacy of death.
  Bibliography: p.
  1. Sanson family. 2. Executions and executioners
—France—History. I. Title.
HV8553.L45   364.6'6'0922 [B]   73-8929
ISBN 0-13-529990-X

For Kay Brown

ACKNOWLEDGMENTS

I am deeply indebted to Monsieur Georges Waltzman of the Paris office of Debevoise, Plimpton, Lyons & Gates, who not only wrote countless letters in my behalf to town halls and record offices all over France, but to the twenty-nine Sansons listed in the Paris telephone directory. His interest and his encouragement were unceasing. My warmest thanks to Maître Jean Jacquinot, Avocat à la Cour and good friend, who was never too busy to answer my queries and to offer help by phone, by letter, and in person. My appreciation and gratitude to Madame Georges Harburger of the Musée de la Préfécture de Police, who gave so generously of her time, and unearthed so many interesting records; and to the staffs of the Bibliothèque Nationale, the Archives Nationale and the Musée Carnavalet, all of whom aided my search. Without the knowledge and resourcefulness of Elizabeth Roth and Roberta Wong of the Print Room at the New York Public Library, I could never have found many of the illustrations I wanted. Thanks, too, to my sister Jessica, who accompanied me on a cold, damp tour of Northern France, visiting towns where the Sansons lived and worked, and to my cousin, Kenneth Straus, who spent a rainy Sunday with me in the Cemetery of Montmartre taking pictures of the Sanson tombstone.

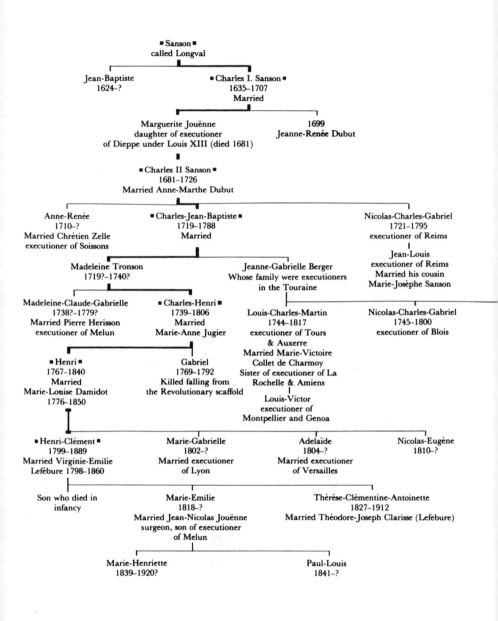

Louis-Cyr-Charlemagne 1748–1794 executioner of Provins Married	Marie-Josèphe 1751–1813 Married Jean-Louis Sanson, executioner of Reims	Pierre Chanks 1753–?	Jean-Baptiste-Pierre 1754–?	Joseph-Claude 1757–1779	Gabrielle
Marie-Madeleine Geneviève Herisson	Marie-Fare-Marguerite Gendron				
3 children dead in infancy	Louis-Henri-Gabriel ?–1874 tried to make a living as a locksmith and failed				

Sansons were themselves or were related to executioners of Etampes, Meaux, Rennes, Orléans, Reims, Abbeville, Versailles, Soissons, Tours, Dieppe, Amiens, La Rochelle, Montpellier, Blois, Melun, Provins, and Lyon

Men, brother men, that after us live
Let not your hearts too hard against us be;
For if some pity of us poor men ye give,
The sooner God shall take of you pity.

The Ballade of the Hanged, by
François Villon.
(Translated by Algernon Charles
Swinburne)

PROLOGUE

Grave number twenty-seven is one of the oldest in the cemetery of Montmartre. The iron railing surrounding it is rusted, the inscription on its modest headstone almost illegible. Tucked away in a narrow alley of the vast cemetery, it is dwarfed by more pretentious neighbors, and the words FAMILLE SANSON are without resonance beside such sonorities as Hector Berlioz and Emile Zola, Théophile Gautier and Stendhal, Jules and Edmond de Goncourt. Passers-by are far more apt to recognize the names engraved on the tombstones of Madame Récamier and Alphonsine Plessis (La Dame aux Camélias) than those of Charles-Henri Sanson or his grandson Henri-Clément.

The weather and the years have obscured the name of Sanson, yet for three centuries, from 1635 to 1889, it was as well known as any in France. Seven generations of Sansons could boast of acquaintance with kings and queens, with princes of the Church and of the Realm, with politicians and writers, bankers and revolutionaries, newspaper editors and royal mistresses. The Sansons were people of importance; feared rather than loved, scorned rather than admired. But from an inauspicious beginning to an ignominious end, the Sanson name is inextricably bound to the history of France.

There are twenty-nine Sansons listed in the 1972 Paris telephone directory, all of whom deny kinship with the family of executioners; the last direct descendant to visit the gravesite was seen and recognized in 1920. Yet in

[1]

May of 1971 and again in May of 1972, two pots of red geraniums were placed on the tombstone. So someone— friend or relative?—remembers; someone knows that the royal executioners were also human beings, and honors them as such.

He was a tall man, taller than most of the townsfolk who stood watching him. And today his height was emphasized, exaggerated by the platform on which he stood. An actor? Perhaps, if one noticed only the regular features, the ash-blond hair that fell to his shoulders, the slim waist and long legs. But the breadth of his shoulders, the strong neck, the powerful muscular arms seemed to indicate a more strenuous profession. Acrobat? Stonemason? Soldier? A closer look revealed more puzzling contrasts: the man's bronzed skin was too young for the lines that furrowed his cheeks, his body too lithe, too healthy to make apology for its presence. Why were his shoulders hunched, why did he suddenly turn his face from the spectators as if in shame?

A huge crowd had gathered, converging on the square from every street and byway for although the man was not a native of Rouen, his name was known. The crowd's appraisal was muted at first, its curiosity temporarily appeased by a study of his physical appearance. But as the wait lengthened, whispered conjecture became impatient grumbling, followed moments later by argument and complaint.

Abusive shouts greeted the appearance of a second man. Hands were clenched, arms raised aloft. An insignificant figure, the newcomer scarcely seemed worthy of the crowd's displeasure. Wearing only a pair of torn breeches, the upper half of his emaciated body bare, his ribs might have been covered by transparent silk rather than flesh.

A third man mounted the platform, and suddenly a hushed stillness enveloped the square.

The presence of Pierre Jouënne always precipitated a silence compounded of hatred, contempt, and fear. Today's silence held the added ingredient of curiosity; for the tall, blond giant with the hunched shoulders was not only Pierre Jouënne's new son-in-law but his new assistant.

Pierre Jouënne was the executioner of Rouen, of Dieppe, and of Caudebec-en-Caux.

This day in 1663 marked the young man's debut, an important day for Charles Sanson, a former adventurer and soldier of the King. His role in this drama might be a minor one, but every eye was upon him. He was dressed like his father-in-law, but his coarse woolen shirt, vest and knee breeches, woolen stockings, and thick-soled boots were a far cry from the colorful attire of a lieutenant in the marquis de la Boissière's regiment. Nervousness might have been the reason for his apologetic stance, yet why should he be nervous? He was expected simply to administer the beating that preceded the victim's true punishment, being broken on the wheel.

Strange that an ex-soldier should pale as he accepted the thick club that was handed him, stranger still that those nearest the scaffold should see beads of sweat spring up across his forehead. He swayed uncertainly for a moment, then staggered forward, only to have his legs fold up beneath him. He fell to the wooden platform, the club clattering down beside his inert body.

An inauspicious beginning for a man who would not

[3]

only occupy the position of royal executioner, but who would found a dynasty of executioners; a man whose sons and grandsons and great-grandsons would follow in his footsteps; whose granddaughters and great-granddaughters would marry executioners; whose brothers and uncles and cousins would wield the axe and the sword, would hang, quarter, burn, brand, mutilate, break on the wheel and ultimately guillotine in every major town and city in France.

The subsequent deeds of the Sanson family were to be well chronicled; but of this, the first Sanson, the official record is brief, stating merely that: "When, having to break [on the wheel] a certain Martin Eslau, executioner Pierre Jouënne ordered his new son-in-law to administer the rod to the victim, the aforementioned son-in-law fainted . . . and was jeered by the crowd."

In *Le Nouveau Paris*, published in 1862, Sébastien Mercier writes that he would like to know what went on in an executioner's mind; whether he looked upon his terrible role as nothing more than an ordinary job; whether he could sleep, knowing he had heard a man's last words, seen the last look in a man's eyes.

Who were the Sansons? To most they were sinister figures; monsters with thick fingers and blood-rimmed fingernails; objects of scorn, fated to be detested, reviled, feared; they were objects, not human beings. Their existence was tolerated, their job accepted as a necessary evil. Had they any feelings at all? Did they love and hate, did they have weaknesses, needs, prejudices, doubts, fears?

What manner of men—proud, vain, ambitious?—embark upon a career of this kind, and then, having lived as pariahs themselves, bestow the same heritage upon their sons?

[4]

An eighteenth-century engraving in the *Almanach des Prisons* shows a man undergoing execution. His hand already has pulled the cord to release the blade of the guillotine, his head already has rolled out onto the scaffold. The man is identified as Sanson, and underneath the engraving is the following verse:

Admirez de Sanson l'intelligence extrême
Par le couteau fatal il a tout fait périr
Dans cet affreux état que va-t-il devenir
Il se guillotine lui-même.

Admire Sanson's profound intelligence
With his fatal blade he has made everything
    perish
In this terrible state of affairs, what can he do
But guillotine himself.

There are several legends regarding the origins of the Sanson family. The most common has it that they were Florentine by birth, that their name was Sansoni (or Sanzoni), and that they came to France in the retinue of Maria de' Medici. Henri-Clément Sanson, the last member of the family to occupy the position of executioner, wrote in his lengthy and questionable account of the family history that: "The first of the Sansons to devote his life to the punishment of the guilty, Pietro Sansoni (for he was Italian) was thrown into this life-work of reprobation because of sentiments heroic for the times in which he lived, and because of a combination of shocking circumstances."

A second tale, perpetuated by one of the Sansons' descendants, claims that the true family coat of arms dates from the time of the Crusades; that a Sanson de Longval was the Seneschal of Robert the Magnificent, father of William the Conqueror. A much later—and more likely—escutcheon displays a cracked bell and the punning motto "San son"—without sound.

A third story relates that the family was established in Abbeville in the fifteenth century and belonged to the rich bourgeoisie. In this version, several Sansons held the office of *échevin,* or municipal magistrate, of Abbeville. One allegedly served at the court of Henri IV, and his grandson, Nicolas Sanson, geographer and teacher of Louis XIV, is purported to be a descendant of Sanson de Longval.

All of these tales contain more mythology (or more accurately, wishful thinking) than fact; and all have undoubtedly come into being for the same reason. The Sansons, filled with repugnance and shame for their bloodstained ancestry, have tried throughout the centuries to exculpate, to exonerate, absolve, compensate, excuse, apologize, atone, elevate, justify, and defend their existence in any way they could think of. Trying to prove a noble heritage was only one of them. However, the surname of Longval establishes them as having come from Picardie, the province where Longval is located, and their appearance in that locale is recorded not in the fifteenth but in the seventeenth century.

The village of Longval (spelled Longueval at that time) consisted of three hundred inhabitants. It was a feudal enclave, paying taxes to the Royal treasury, to the

Church, and to a man named Sanson, who was nothing more than a vassal of the local seigneur. But because he pocketed one third of the village revenue, he elected to call himself Sanson de Longueval, a name implying nobility. In actual fact, he resided in Abbeville, a rich commercial town on the Somme river about eighty kilometers from Longueval and only twenty kilometers from the sea. Abbeville was not only a center for the manufacture of cloth, but also a busy port where the wealthy bourgeois dealt in fish, wine, animal skins, oriental spices, wood, cotton, and many other domestic and foreign commodities. With his revenues from Longueval, Sanson invested in some of these profitable ventures and managed to make a very comfortable living.

It is known that he married a Mademoiselle Brossier, and that they had two sons: Jean-Baptiste, born in 1624, and Charles, in 1635. The boys were very young when both parents died in an epidemic, and they were brought up by their maternal uncle, Pierre Brossier, a local magistrate who held title to the fief of Limeux.

Brossier's daughter, Colombe, was exactly the same age as Charles, and it is said that they loved each other from earliest childhood. Jean-Baptiste, older by eleven years, studied for and attained the title of magistrate, whereupon his uncle not only obtained for him the position of Councillor of the Court of Abbeville, but also informed him that he was to marry Colombe.

Whether Brossier knew of Charles's feelings for his daughter and sent him away, or whether the young man's broken heart was the cause of his departure is not known. But Charles left Abbeville and set out for Paris, determined to offer his services to the Crown. It is thought that he joined the royal fleet at Rochefort and set sail for Québec, where he spent three years in the King's service. Upon returning to France he disembarked at Toulon where he found a message from Colombe asking for help.

In Abbeville, Pierre Brossier was dead and Jean-Baptiste, now married to Colombe, was an invalid. The fief of Limeux, bequeathed to Colombe, had been taken back by the local seigneur, and the legal procedures undertaken by Jean-Baptiste to recover possession of it had emptied his bank account and compelled him to sell his house. Probably as a result of this misfortune, Jean-Baptiste had suffered a stroke which left him paralyzed and blind. Charles, comparatively wealthy with the money he had earned in the New World, supported the couple as best he could. But in 1661, unable to trust his emotions if he continued to live under the same roof as Colombe, he suddenly gave her the major part of his savings and purchased a lieutenancy in the regiment of the marquis de la Boissière, Lieutenant of the King and His Majesty's governor for the town of Dieppe.

One year later, Charles received word that Jean-Baptiste had died and that Colombe, a widow without funds, had left Abbeville and was journeying to Dieppe to meet him. He arranged to accompany her on the last leg of her journey, and as they were riding toward Dieppe, a violent storm erupted. Frightened by a bolt of lightning, their horse shied, bolted, and threw them both to the ground. When Charles regained consciousness, he found a man, a woman, and a young girl bending over him. They informed him that Colombe was dead.

Until he was well enough to return to his regiment, the family, Jouënne by name, looked after him—or rather Marguerite Jouënne looked after him, and it wasn't long before he had fallen in love with her. She consented to

[8]

become his mistress, but stubbornly and inexplicably refused to marry him. One day, crossing the main square of Dieppe, he caught sight of a scaffold, and standing beside it a tall, bearded man. Horrified, Charles recognized Marguerite's father, Pierre Jouënne, the executioner of Dieppe, Rouen, and Caudebec-en-Caux, and he realized with a sinking heart why the girl could not accept his proposal of marriage.

Although prejudice against executioners would increase immeasurably with the advent of the Revolution over a hundred years later, it had always existed, especially in provincial towns and villages. Daughters of executioners were forbidden to marry men outside the profession. It is said that when an executioner's family had a marriageable daughter, they were required to affix a document to their front door stating the fact, thereby protecting the young men of the town from an encounter, much less an involvement, with so tainted a blood line. Executioners' orders, letters of commission, payments, and other communiqués were not supposed to be delivered into their hands, but thrown to the ground so that the recipients would have to kneel to receive the missive. Executioners were often required to live in isolated places, and some communities decreed that their houses had to be painted red. In church, the executioner's pew was usually set apart from the others. As public prejudice increased, some executioners could find no lodgings, and merchants frequently refused to sell to them, fearing that other customers would be frightened away from their shops.

Charles Sanson must have realized what would happen, because he made an effort to stay away from the Jouënne farm. But his feelings were evidently stronger than his will. Small towns being what they always have

[9]

been, it didn't take long for word of the liaison to reach headquarters. The marquis de la Boissière accused his lieutenant of dishonoring the regiment and ordered him either to stop seeing Marguerite or to resign his commission. Charles left the barracks and returned to the Jouënne farm, only to find himself threatened by Pierre: either he married Marguerite or Pierre, her own father, would have to kill her. Charles Sanson resigned his commission and married her. (Subsequently, he would learn that the Jouënne name was well known in Normandie, for all the men in the family were executioners.)

And so the first Sanson entered the profession that would belong to every member of his family for six generations to come. His career was not chosen, but forced upon him—a heavy penalty for having fallen in love.

If the concept of justice in the centuries preceding the Revolution seems neither just nor humane to a contemporary mind, it was nonetheless consistent with an age when Church and State were one, and when "justice" meant the Justice of God. It was dispensed in the name of the King, who ruled by Divine Right as the instrument of God. Punishment of the guilty was God's will; therefore in the eyes of Church and Sovereign, punishment glorified the Creator. This justice, which sanctioned the most barbaric forms of torture, had prevailed since the Middle Ages and would continue to exist for as long as the people believed in the absolute authority of the Church and maintained a blind faith in its teachings.

France would remain a feudal society until 1789, a country divided into provinces, sectors ruled by wealthy and powerful aristocrats who enjoyed enormous privilege and whose authority was absolute. Princes of the Realm and Princes of the Church (many had inherited or acquired both titles) owned not only the land but the people on it. Each province made and administered its own laws, and laws differed from province to province.

At the beginning of the eighteenth century, law courts had to wrestle with some three hundred and sixty different codes. An offense punishable in one province by a fine might result in branding or even death in another. But a nobleman anywhere could commit almost any crime without risk of prison or torture, whereas a bourgeois or peasant received severe punishment for the slightest offense. Trial by jury did not exist; prisoners were questioned by a judge, who also imposed the sentence if he had sufficient evidence to convict a man. If the evidence was not sufficient, he was permitted to use torture to obtain a confession.

And torture was an accepted form of punishment: "For he that hath suffered in the flesh hath ceased from sin," said the Holy Scriptures (I Peter 4.1). Frenchmen believed and obeyed.

Charles Sanson was a God-fearing man and a church-goer. But although he became inured to his servitude and resigned to an inescapable profession, the marks of shame and humiliation were engraved on his face, his torment manifest in an increasing moodiness of his character. The Church made its pronouncements, the red-robed justices

[11]

of the courts mouthed their decrees and sentences, but his was the nightmarish task of seeing that their ideas and words became reality.

Reality assumed a variety of forms, the severity of which depended upon the crime committed. The pillory —literally a post or pillar to which criminals were chained—consisted in Paris of an octagonal tower with a ground floor and one landing. The culprit was exhibited during three consecutive market days, taken around the pillory at half hour intervals so that he could be seen from all sides. In some towns (Orléans for one) the prisoner was made to stand up in a cage that revolved on a pivot. This was a common method of punishment for such crimes as bankruptcy, forgery, bigamy, fraud, cheating at cards, robbery of fruit and vegetables, sale of prohibited books, and blasphemy. The *carcan,* an iron collar riveted about the neck of the victim, sometimes was used as an adjunct to the pillory. Hung over it was a placard, giving the man's name and the crime with which he was charged. The *amende honorable,* frequently a preliminary step to a more drastic punishment, might mean parading a prisoner through the streets in a cart, or in early centuries, breaking a knight's spurs on a dunghill. In the case of a soldier it consisted of degrading him by breaking his shield in three pieces with a hammer and pouring a basin of hot water over his head; a nobleman would be stripped of his sword. Flagellation (abolished for the civilian population in 1789 but continued in the French Navy until 1848) and mutilation (branding with a red-hot iron or amputating a hand, a foot, an ear, the tongue) were common punishments administered by the executioner.

Essorillement, or ear-cropping, was another frequent punishment. For a first offense, one ear would be severed;

if the culprit was found guilty for the second time, the other ear would follow. The left ear usually was cut first, because of a belief that it was connected with the sexual organs. Its absence, therefore, would prevent procreation of children who might inherit the father's criminal tendencies. *Tenaillement* condemned a victim to have the skin stripped from his body with red-hot tongs or pincers, after which hot lead or wax or resin would be poured onto the wounds. The rack, a frame with a roller at each end, was a device to which the victim was attached by his wrists and ankles. As the frame rotated, his joints were stretched, his limbs usually dislocated.

Before the advent of the guillotine, the death penalty varied, depending not only upon the crime committed but also upon a man's or a woman's position in society. Burning at the stake was reserved largely for Jews, Protestants, and other heretics. Decapitation with a sword was a privilege reserved for the nobility, whereas commoners were beheaded with an axe. Vagabonds, pickpockets, petty thieves, and culprits of the lowliest variety met their fate by the hangman's noose. In quartering (reserved almost exclusively for parricides), the convict was tied by his arms and legs to four horses, each of which was then driven in a different direction.

Breaking on the wheel was a form of punishment said to have originated in Germany. The victim was placed on a cart wheel, his limbs stretched out along the spokes. As the wheel revolved, the executioner broke his bones by striking him with an iron bar. In France the guilty man usually was strangled after the second or third blow, but other countries did not shorten suffering in this manner. *Estrapade* was a method whereby the victim was dropped from a great height; when this occurred on shipboard it was termed *la cale* and it existed in two forms—*la cale sèche,* meaning that the man was dropped onto the deck, and *la cale humide,* into the water. A death sentence also could mean drowning, being flayed alive, or being boiled in oil or water.

Charles Sanson may not have used all of these refinements, but it is known that he broke Claude Vautier on the wheel for theft and murder, and that he meted out the same punishment to Jean Nouis, convicted of the same crimes. He severed the fist of Urbaine Attibard, a young woman of thirty-five who had been convicted of poisoning her husband: subsequently he hanged her.

The years in Rouen and Dieppe were hard ones, and tragedy struck a personal blow in 1681 when Marguerite died after giving birth to a son, who was also named Charles. In 1685 Charles Sanson, widower, left Dieppe and went to Paris.

His activities during a two-year period are not known, but in all probability the only work he could have found would have been that of executioner's assistant. In 1687 the *bourreau* (hangman or executioner) of Paris, Nicolas Levasseur, called La Rivière, was stripped of his office and ordered to sell his commission because he had been proved guilty of levying a tax on prostitutes—a privilege enjoyed legally by the executioner of Orléans, but not by the one in Paris. Because Nicolas Levasseur's wife had been a Joüenne and a cousin of Marguerite's, the Joüenne family knew of the impending vacancy. None of them could afford the price that Levasseur was asking, but apparently Charles Sanson had the money, wanted the position, and bought it. His *Lettre de Provision,* which follows, is in the National Archives in Paris.

EXECUTER DES ARRÊTS

Et Sentences Criminelles
à Paris, 1688.

Louis, by the grace of God King of France and
Navarre, to all those who shall see these presents,
greetings! By order of our Court of the Parlement
of Paris, the eleventh August of the present year,
it having been ordained for the reasons
hereinafter set out that Charles Sanson known as
Longval shall alone fulfil the office of Executioner
of High Justice in our city, provostry and
viscounty of Paris subject to his obtaining our
letters patent for the said office; wherefore be it
known that in view of the good account given us
of the said Charles Sanson known as Longval, we
have, in accordance with the said order, given
and granted, and do by these presents give and
grant him the status of Executioner of the High
Works and Criminal Sentences in our aforesaid
city, provostry and viscounty of Paris, heretofore
held and exercised by Nicolas Levasseur, known
as La Rivière, last incumbent thereof, the same
having been discharged by the said order of our
said Court of the Parlement of Paris, and added,
under the counterseal of our Chancery, in respect
of the said office and its tenure, future exercise,
enjoyment and use by the aforesaid Sanson, to the
rights of levy in the fairs and markets of our said
city, provostry and viscounty of Paris, products,
gains, revenues and emoluments, such and similar
as have well and properly been enjoyed by the
incumbents of like offices; to wit: enjoyment of the
house and habitation of the *Pillori des Halles*, its
appurtenances and dependencies without let or

[15]

hindrance for whatsoever cause, and furthermore
the right to exact from each merchant bearing
eggs on his back or by hand one egg, from each
saddle-load two eggs, from each cartload, a
demi-quarteron, and from each basket of apples,
pears, grapes and other produce whether arriving
by land or by water in boats carrying the same
load as a horse one *sou*; for each laden horse the
same amount and for each cart two *sous*; for those
bringing whether by land or by water, green peas,
medlars, hemp-seed, mustard-seed, poulavin,
millet, walnuts, chestnuts, hazelnuts his spoonful
as has always been the custom; from each
itinerant merchant bringing on his back or by
hand butter, cheese, poultry and fresh-water fish,
six deniers; for each horse, one *sou*; for each
cartload of beans, two *sous*; for each tip-cart
twenty *sous* and a carp; and for each bag of peas
or broad beans in pods one *sou*, and for each
basket six *deniers*; and for each case of oranges and
lemons brought in by itinerant merchants either
by water or by land, one *sou*; for each wagonload
of oysters in the shell one *quarteron* and for each
boatload in proportion and for every person
bringing brooms, one broom; for every horse-load,
two; and for every cartload six; for every
merchant bringing in coal, his potful; from the
sworn ropemakers, rope for the executions; all of
which rights have always been levied both in our
own city of Paris and in other parts of our
Kingdom, which the said Sanson will enjoy, as
also exemption from all levies in respect of
nightwatch, guards, bridges, ferries, receipt of
wine and other beverages for his own provender,
with the right to carry arms both offensive and
defensive, himself and his servants, on account of
his office. . . .

Bestowed at Versailles, the 23rd day of
September, in the year of grace 1688, the 46th
year of our reign.

The rights and privileges enumerated in this curious
document date back to the fifteenth century. Then, as in
1688 when Charles Sanson received his royal commission, neither the executioner of Paris nor any of his
counterparts in other sectors of the kingdom received a
fixed salary. Instead, an ordinance issued in 1495 by
Charles VIII entitled them to what was termed the *droit
de havage*. *Havage*, from the verb *havir*, today means to
scorch or burn, to go through fire, but in those days it
meant to take with the hands. (Today's verb *avoir* derives
from it.) *Havage* meant that the executioner could
physically pick up from the various fairs and markets in
Paris eggs, fruit, fish, vegetables, coal, wood, and all of
the other items specified in the king's letters-patent and
either keep them for his own use or sell them. If the
executioner had been permitted only to fill his hands, his
total *havage* wouldn't have amounted to very much; but
the executioner was allowed an additional bonus—his
assistants could help him. And no law regulated the
number of assistants he could claim. The well known
French expression *"insolent comme un valet de bourreau"*
(brash as a hangman's aide) dates from that period.

In addition to *havage*, the executioner had the right to
all clothing and effects found on the bodies of men and
women he had put to death. He himself paid no taxes,
and it is estimated that he could net as much as 65,000
livres a year. He had to pay his assistants—fifteen to
twenty of them—and look after his horses, but his rope,
his whips, his axes, sabers, swords, all the tools of his

[17]

trade were given to him by the various corporations. His house, called La Maison du Pilori des Halles, belonged to the State, but he lived in it rent-free, and as the name indicates, it was adjacent to the pillory and near the markets.

In addition to these sources of revenue, Charles Sanson soon discovered another method of earning money, one which would continue to be employed by all of his descendants. As executioner of Paris, one of his duties was to bring the bodies of victims not claimed by their families to his house after execution and keep them until the clergy had decided where they were to be buried. This necessitated his keeping one room in the house to be used as a morgue. Horrified when he first learned of this stipulation, Charles finally let his sense of guilt conquer his disgust and began studying the cadavers with the thought that he might be able to assuage pain as well as inflict it. He bought books on surgery and medicine, studied the bones, muscles, the articulation of the joints, and began to concoct remedies. He mixed creams and balms to ease the ache of rheumatism, he set broken bones, mended torn flesh, and seemingly became expert at the healing art. Hearing of his skill, people began consulting him, their inborn fear of the executioner tempered by their hope that he could help them.

His day was a busy one. In the morning, flagellation usually preceded the victim's hours in the pillory, and of course crowds gathered to watch and jeer, to throw stones and pelt the culprit with garbage. Afterward Charles and his assistants took their carriage and drove to the Châtelet or to some other prison to pick up those condemned to death and convey them to the place de Grève for execution. On those days, Charles dressed in his official uniform—a red singlet with the gallows em-

[18]

broidered across his chest in black, and a ladder embroidered across his back. His culottes were of royal blue.

When Charles's appointment as royal executioner became official, his son young Charles was seven years old. A priest taught the boy to read and write and instructed him in mathematics, history, and catechism. But the child had no playmates because no one would let his offspring consort with the son of the executioner. Concerned about the boy's loneliness and worried too because the scourging of women, the flaying of bigamists, the public exhibition of prostitutes—and the crowds that gathered to watch—created tremendous noise and turmoil, Charles bought a house near the church of Saint-Laurent, in what is today the Faubourg Poissonnière. This removed his son from the proximity of the pillory and gave father and son a semblance of respectability. The house had a garden and outbuildings to house his assistants, his carriages, horses, and the tools of his trade.

But respectability would never be more than an illusion to Charles Sanson. In the *Mémoires* edited by Henri Sanson and published in the nineteenth century, there is a confession attributed to Charles, written in Paris in 1693, just five years after he had assumed the burden of being royal headsman and six years before he would retire:

> God in his infinite goodness, measured on our shoulders the cross He wished us to bear, [says the unhappy executioner]. There is no misfortune, however heavy, to which one cannot be reconciled; and what at first appears to us as impossible for a man to accomplish as it is for him to swallow all the waters of the ocean, comes to

pass by the mere strength of habit. After entering into rebellion against my fate, I have been led to suffer patiently the evil I did not deserve as well as the consequences of my impudence, praying that my death should be less tainted than my life . . . and before asking for God's mercy, I wish to confess my sins and to state the reasons that led me to adopt the miserable profession of executioner so that they [my children] may forgive me if I deserve forgiveness. . . .

The confession goes on to tell of his years as a lieutenant in the marquis de la Boissière's regiment and to explain the circumstances responsible for his loathed title.

Trapped and desperately ashamed of his daily tasks, Charles was nonetheless a realist about his son's future and knew the boy had no choice except to follow in his father's footsteps. Young Charles was sent to serve an apprenticeship with the executioner of Pontoise.

In June of 1699, he returned to Paris and assisted his father in what would be the sixty-four-year-old executioner's last appearance on the scaffold.

The affair concerned Madame Angélique Tiquet, the wife of a magistrate and councillor of the Parlement of Paris. Tired of her husband's avarice, brutality, and infidelities, Angélique plotted to poison him, then changed her mind and hired assassins to murder him in a deserted street. At the last minute she had had another change of heart and canceled the order, but Tiquet's suspicions plus the voluntary confession of one of the assassins resulted in her arrest. She was sentenced to be decapitated in the place de Grève.

Several factors contributed to Charles *père*'s violent reaction to this particular execution. First of all, he had

had more than his share of torturing, hanging, and decapitating. He was tired, frightened, and disgusted. Secondly, Angélique Tiquet bore an uncanny resemblance to Colombe—the same coloring, the same shade of hair, the same figure. To add to Charles Sanson's misery, the day of execution was suffocatingly hot, and as he stood on the scaffold, listening to the Abbé de la Chétârdie, Angélique's confessor, the sky darkened and thunder rumbled in the distance—another reminder of Colombe and the day of her death.

Suddenly Paris was deluged by torrential rains. The crowd that had gathered in front of the Hôtel de Ville dispersed, the executioner's assistants sought shelter under the scaffold, and Charles found himself alone with the priest and Angélique.

"Please forgive me," Charles said to her. "I am sorry that you will have to wait; but if I tried to execute you during this downpour my saber might slip and cause you undue suffering." (Being of the privileged class, Angélique was permitted to be executed with a sword rather than an axe.)

He waited for over an hour, pity for the poor woman consuming him as he looked at her delicate body, more sharply outlined as her clothing clung to it, at her tangled hair, at the pale face so like Colombe's. At last the rain stopped, the crowd began to emerge from doorways and from under balconies, and Charles realized he could no longer postpone the inevitable.

"It's time," he said, then added gently, "Please forgive me, madame."

The unexpected apology no less than the sincerity in his voice brought tears to the victim's eyes. She took his hand and kissed it.

It was then that Charles Sanson, overcome with

On April 12, 1707, eight days before the death of his father, Charles fils married Anne-Marthe Dubut, his stepmother's sister, in the church of Notre Dame de Bonne Nouvelle. In 1703, at the time of his father's retirement to Brie-Comte-Robert, the young man had been given the provisional title of executioner; in 1707, after the death of his father, he received his commission from the King.

Young Charles was twenty-six, his bride twenty-four; and after a few months of living with his father's widow, the young couple purchased their own house situated at the corner of the rue Poissonnière (today the Faubourg Poissonnière) and the rue d'Enfer (today more prosaically named the rue Bleue) in the parish of Saint-Pierre de Montmartre. This dwelling, for which he paid six thousand livres in 1707, would remain in the Sanson family until 1778 when it was sold for one hundred thousand.

A pragmatist in matters concerning his profession, Charles thought it quite normal and natural that the son and grandson of executioners should be an executioner himself. However, he had inherited both his father's sensitivity and the gentle character of Marguerite Jouënne. To the end of his life, he enjoyed the reputation of being kind and merciful to his victims. Except for Madame Tiquet, the first part of his career brought only thieves and brigands to the scaffold, but after the death of Louis XIV in 1715, the type of his victims changed.

France was in a precarious condition. Wars had depleted the treasury, and the Revocation of the Edict of Nantes in 1685 had sent many industrial bourgeois (many of whom were Protestant) out of the country. In order to secure funds, Philippe d'Orléans, the Regent, went after the fortunes of Protestant bankers, questioning not only the origins of their money but their right to it. Many were condemned to the galleys so that he could confiscate their fortunes. Charles executed the ten richest and most prominent.

In 1716 Anne-Marthe gave birth to a daughter, Anne-Renée, who would latter marry Christian Zelle, the executioner of Soissons. In that year, too, Charles had a most unusual experience—at least for an executioner. He was instrumental in saving the life of one of his victims.

Antoinette Sicard, a very beautiful woman in her thirties, was the mistress of a German named von Schlieben who in turn was involved in a plot to murder the Regent. Antoinette's neighbors averred that she received a great many male visitors, but in reality the men were all one man—von Schlieben, disguised variously as an officer, a shopkeeper, and a priest in order to confuse anyone who might be following him. One evening, her neighbors heard voices raised in anger, followed by the sound of objects hitting walls and floors. They called the guard. The door was broken down and she was seen confronting a man wearing the uniform of a musketeer. It was von Schlieben, who promptly took advantage of the ensuing mêlée to escape. Antoinette, on evidence given by her neighbors, was arrested as a prostitute.

[25]

Because of her lover's involvement in the plot to murder Philippe d'Orléans, she could not reveal the true story and was condemned to receive thirty lashes with the cat-o'-nine-tails on her back, to undergo an hour of public exhibition in the pillory, and then to be imprisoned in the Salpetrière—which was certainly far more efficient at enforcing chastity than saltpeter could be—for an indefinite period of time.

One of Charles Sanson's aides stole a ring from her while conveying her from pillory to prison. Seeing it on the man's finger, Charles took it to the police, whereupon the entire tale of the plot emerged. The guilty were punished, and Antoinette released from prison. In gratitude, she gave the ring to Charles, whose descendants showed it proudly—as proof of their loyalty to the Crown.

This was also the year in which Philippe d'Orléans, in a desperate attempt to cure France's financial ills, fell prey to the theories of the Scotsman, John Law. The Regent authorized Law's bank to issue paper money, henceforth to be accepted as legal currency; and at the same time he gave the financier leave to issue stock in the Mississippi Company, which reputedly owned vast wealth in the New World. Intrigued by this new system of banking, Frenchmen invested heavily in Law's scheme. When the stock company was merged with the Royal bank in 1720, speculation ran riot. The stock rose in price from five hundred to twenty thousand livres and the number of banknotes in circulation increased to three billion. But this gambler's paradise was not destined to last; an attempt to devalue the paper currency damaged the public confidence, and the entire system collapsed as suddenly as it had risen. As is frequent in such debacles, well-informed speculators such as the duc de Bourbon

[26]

and the Prince de Conti sold their stock at huge profit, but thousands of tradesmen and country folk and even household servants were ruined. Whether or not Charles Sanson suffered financially is not known, but he and his successors inherited the terrible legacy of suffering and punishment that follows crises of any description.

Comte Antoine de Horn (or de Hoorne) of Flanders, grandson of the Prince de Ligne and cousin of the Regent, confronted a man in a cabaret one evening on the pretext of wanting to buy shares from him, stabbed him to death, and stole his pocketbook. De Horn escaped with his companion, the Chevalier de Mille, but not before they had been seen and recognized by one of the valets in the café. Arrested, they confessed, de Horn adding that the crime was excusable because his victim was a Jew. Despite appeals for clemency by many members of the nobility, Philippe d'Orléans refused to pardon the culprits and they were condemned to die on the wheel.

References to the death of the young, good-looking comte de Horn are frequent in the annals of the eighteenth century. Among others, that inveterate gossip, letter-writer, and mother of the Regent, the Princess Palatine, speaks of it in a letter to one of her friends:

> Paris, 31 March 1720. I think the devil must
> have been set loose this year with all this
> murdering. Not a single night passes without
> people being found murdered for their *billets de
> banque*. People of high quality are dabbling in this
> ugly and dreadful trade, amongst others that
> young, good-looking comte de Hoorne of
> Flanders. The Comte was only twenty-three, M.
> de Mortagne my *chevalier d'honneur*, who had

[27]

presented him to me about three weeks ago, died
in his bed last Monday, and on Tuesday the
Comte died on the wheel. It makes one sad. All
France begged for mercy for the Comte, but my
son said that for such an abominable deed an
example had to be made, which duly happened,
to the great satisfaction of the *peuple*, who cried
"Notre Regent est juste!" (*Letters from Liselotte*,
translated by Maria Kroll.)

Elizabeth-Charlotte, Princess Palatine was reputed to
know where the wind was blowing, but not even she
knew the identity of one person who interceded for the
luckless comte de Horn. On the night of March 23, 1720,
Charles Sanson was walking in the park when he was
approached by a veiled woman who pleaded with him to
save the life of the twenty-three-year-old victim. The
woman, after pleading in vain, lifted her veil, revealing
herself to be Madame de Parabère, the Regent's mistress.
She tried to bribe the executioner—to no avail. But
Charles finally agreed that if her friends made an
attempt to kidnap de Horn while he was en route to the
gallows, nothing would be done to stop it. If they failed,
they failed. All Charles could promise was that he would
try to send her some souvenir of de Horn's clothing.

It was customary for the executioner to receive written
instructions both as to the method of execution and any
refinements that were to precede it. When Charles was
informed that de Horn was to be broken on the wheel, he
looked for the usual additional permission to use the
retentum—a very thin rope, invisible to the public, with
which the executioner strangled his victim before subjecting him to the torture of the wheel. There was no
mention of it. Appalled by the barbarism of his orders,

[28]

Charles Sanson disobeyed them and used the *retentum* anyway. He also kept his promise to Madame de Parabère and sent her a lock of de Horn's hair.

Barely a year later, the wheel would be used again, this time on a man at the opposite end of the social scale from Comte Antoine de Horn, but whose name was far better known. Louis Dominique Cartouche, bandit, pickpocket, and assassin, was just four and a half feet tall. Born in Paris in 1663, he was the oldest of five children whose father was a cooper in the rue Pont-aux-Choux. A typical Parisian *gamin*, he never learned to read or write, but an innate intelligence and abundant inventiveness plus shrewdness and cunning acquired in the streets and at the Foire de Saint-Laurent soon made him the leader of a large gang. Five years spent with a caravan of gypsies added to his repertoire of card tricks and developed his inborn agility. It was said that he could jump from one rooftop to another as easily as a monkey.

Gay, insouciant, joyous, he was reputed to be a marvelous raconteur, and it was said that no woman could resist the twinkle in his huge black eyes, his smiling mouth, his incredible charm. His agents came from all classes of society. They stole from the Palais Royal and the Louvre, from banks and shops and private houses, they robbed coaches on the highways and ships in the harbors. And because so many people—particularly proprietors of cafés, taverns, and wayside inns—gave him shelter, he managed to elude capture for many years.

Even after he was betrayed by a man called Duchâtelet, who had promised to hand him over to the authorities in return for personal amnesty, it took thirty soldiers to trap the bandit and convey him to the prison of the Grande Châtelet. He was put into a cell with triple doors and chained to an iron stake, but he had friends even among the jailers. An attempted escape almost succeeded. After that he was transferred to the impregnable and dreaded Conciergerie and sentenced to be tortured—placed on a cross of St. Andrew and beaten with an iron bar—before being broken on the wheel.

Barbier's *Journal* describes the event, which took place on Friday the 27th of November, 1721:

> All night long [on Thursday the 26th] fiacres carried passengers to the place de Grève, until it was jammed with people, all waiting for the event. Windows facing the square were lit all night. The cold was biting, but the crowd lit fires right in the square, and local merchants sold food and drink. Everyone was laughing, drinking, singing . . . most of the spectators had had their places reserved for over a month.

Barbier adds that after the execution, one of the executioner's assistants kept the cadaver of Cartouche in his house and showed it to the curious, for one *sou* per person.

That took place in November; in July of the following year, five of Cartouche's mistresses were hanged. One of them, under torture, made a full confession revealing the names of sixty of his accomplices, among them several prominent jewelers. The bandit had tried to exonerate members of his own family, but one of his younger brothers, aged fifteen, was caught and sentenced to be hung by his arms for two hours in the place de Grève, a sentence so shocking to Charles Sanson that the executioner cut him down long before the time had expired.

The place de Grève, now the place de l'Hôtel de Ville,

was the site most frequently used for executions. There were other locales—Les Halles, La Place Maubert, the Parvis of Notre Dame, the Pont Neuf, the Pont Saint-Michel, and the Portes of Saint-Antoine, Saint-Honoré, Saint-Denis, and Saint-Jacques—but these were allocated to less stringent penalties.

Called the place de Grève because of the gravel washed up on its sloping banks by the Seine during the earlier centuries, it was then the gathering spot for men who were out of work: odd-job men, laborers of all kinds, especially stonemasons who lived nearby in the old rue de la Mortellerie. Parisians sneeringly called these people "Anges de Grève" and it was said that those seeking work *"faisaient la grève"* or *"se mettaient en grève"* when they could not come to terms with prospective employers. Hence today's meaning of the word—a work stoppage or strike. Until the Revolution, the work of the Sansons took them almost exclusively to this large, imposing square, where such notorious regicides as Montgomery and Ravaillac had met their fate, and where hundreds would follow them in years to come.

Except for the birth of his second son, Nicolas-Charles-Gabriel, the year 1721 would have to be considered an unfortunate one for Charles Sanson. (His oldest son, Charles-Jean-Baptiste, had been born two years earlier.) In October, Philippe d'Orléans abolished the *droit de havage* and replaced it by giving the executioner a salary of sixteen thousand livres a year. This proved a terrible blow to Charles Sanson, who had been accustomed to an income of well over sixty thousand. He demanded and received an audience with the Regent to plead for his rights. But Philippe had already signed the order and refused to rescind it. To pacify the executioner he gave him stock certificates on John Law's bank, in the amount

[31]

of fifty thousand livres, which of course had no value whatsoever. And when Charles Sanson cried out in protest, the Regent merely shrugged, saying that the stock would regain its value someday. Philippe d'Orléans' only concession was to allow the executioner the right to *all* the effects found on the person of the condemned man; heretofore he'd had the right to only those articles found above the belt. Charles also obtained the right to a fee of five *sous* per execution, a ridiculously small stipend. However, he did supplement his income, as had his father, with the practice of medicine.

The next five years saw the gradual decline in health that would lead him to resign his commission at the age of forty-five. In May of 1726 he arose from a sickbed to execute Etienne Benjamin des Chauffours for homosexuality, considered a crime despite the fact that the Regent's father was a homosexual. If des Chauffours had been discreet, he might have escaped the ghastly penalty of being burned at the stake; but unfortunately the police found a list of over two hundred men of the nobility who were involved with him. All two hundred could not be executed, so des Chauffours was condemned as the procurer.

In August, Charles Sanson sent in his resignation, asking at the same time that his oldest son might succeed him.

Of all the Sansons, Charles was the only one whose profession did not haunt, embarrass, or shame him. He accepted it; and being a gentle man, he performed his disagreeable duties as mercifully as possible. The fact that his sons had to follow in his footsteps was undeniable, and in view of that fact he deemed it imperative that the older of the two obtain the royal mandate. But the job was not hereditary; the derisive title of Monsieur de Paris given to the executioner of the capital city by the populace would not come to a seven-year-old Charles-Jean-Baptiste without effort. So, as he lay dying, Charles had his wife Marthe call Maître Dupuis, a notary at the Châtelet prison, and two friends, François Prud'homme and Jules Tronson, official questioners. With the latter as witnesses, he bequeathed his job to his son, requesting that Tronson act as the boy's tutor and Prud'homme as interim executioner until the child came of age.

On September 25th, he died and was buried beside his father beneath the church of Saint-Laurent. After a respectable mourning period, his widow remarried, and it is interesting to note that not even the women connected with the Sanson family could escape their fate. Her second husband belonged to a family of executioners from the town of Metz.

If Charles had outlived his wife, the Sanson heritage might not have been such a bloody one. If his gentle stepmother, Renée Dubut, had been able to influence him, the future might have been changed for the generations to come. But Renée was only Jean-Baptiste's grandmother; despite her pleading, it was his mother's will that prevailed. And to Marthe Dubut Sanson, a royal commission was a prized possession, the job of executioner as important to France as any other in the royal household. Renée urged her to take advantage of the child's youth, to use it as an excuse to renounce the inheritance, but Marthe was adamant. Apprehensive that the Parlement might not accept her husband's last will as valid, she decided to plead her cause in person. A tragic figure in her widow's weeds—and fully aware of it—she confronted the Public Prosecutor, whose sympathy (or disgust) made him succumb to her plea and name the seven-year-old Jean-Baptiste executioner. Although a deputy actually carried out the sentence, the seven-year-old child had to legalize every execution by his presence!

[33]

Marthe did not apprentice her offspring to a provincial executioner, but trained them herself. (Anne-Renée would marry the executioner of Soissons; Gabriel became executioner of Reims.) To prepare Jean-Baptiste for his position as Monsieur de Paris he was made to witness flagellation, branding, hanging, decapitation, and breaking on the wheel; at eighteen he performed his first execution, much to his mother's proud joy.

Unfortunately for Marthe, however, Jean-Baptiste never lived up to her hopes. A sensitive man, he suffered deeply; after every execution he became so upset that he would saddle his horse and gallop out of Paris, often riding for hours trying to forget what he had done. Like his grandfather, the ghosts of his victims never left him.

In 1738 Jean-Baptiste married Jules Tronson's daughter Madeleine in the church of Saint-Laurent, and a party to celebrate the wedding was held that evening. The festivities had barely started when Paris was deluged by torrential rains. With many seeking shelter from the storm, no one was particularly surprised to hear a loud knocking at the door.

Three young noblemen stood under the porte-cochère, one wearing the uniform of the Royal Irish guards, the regiment of the comte de Dillon. Without asking their host's name, they accepted his hospitality and entered into the celebration with abandon. Not until the end of the evening did they inquire as to the identity of their kind benefactor, and paled visibly when they learned who he was. The young officer expressed interest in the executioner's arsenal, and asked if he might be permitted to see the various instruments used for torture and for execution. Jean-Baptiste obliged him watching him run his finger along the blade of a double-edged sword to test its sharpness.

[34]

"With a weapon such as this," said the guardsman, "you can no doubt cut off a head with one blow."

Jean-Baptiste nodded.

"If the occasion should ever arise for me," said the officer with a smile, "I shall hold you to your promise."

The officer's name was Comte Thomas-Arthur de Lally baron de Tollendal. And years later, long after his son had taken over his duties, Jean-Baptiste would remember his promise and come out of retirement to honor it.

As the years passed he managed to quell if not to conquer his early anguish. And outwardly at least, he began to resemble his mother, his public countenance hard, rigid, puritanical. Revulsion gave way to resignation; he accepted the job, persuading himself that it was the will of God.

He had two children by Madeleine Tronson: a daughter, Madeleine-Claude-Gabrielle, who married Pierre Hérisson, executioner of Melun (and whose daughter would marry her uncle, Louis-Cyr-Charlemagne Sanson) and a son, Charles-Henri, called "Le Grand," who would succeed his father and become the most famous member of the family because of his activities during the Revolution.

After the death of his first wife, Jean-Baptiste married again, and another link was formed in the chain of executioners that would ultimately stretch the length and breadth of France. His second wife, Jeanne-Gabrielle Berger, belonged to a family of executioners from the province of Touraine. This union would produce six boys and two girls who in turn would enter the confraternity of executioners. The oldest boy, Louis-Charles-Martin, began his career by helping his half-brother Charles-Henri in Paris, and was then named executioner of

Tours, where he plied his trade for twenty-eight years. He retired in September of 1796, but two years later, finding himself without means of support, he applied for the position of executioner of Blois and of Versailles. Both posts were given to others. He finally obtained the appointment in Dijon, and in 1807 was named executioner of Auxerre.

The second son, Nicolas-Charles-Gabriel, began his career in Paris just as his brother had done. He later secured the position of executioner of Blois and then of Montpellier. His predecessor in the latter post, Gilles-Martin Berger, was a drunkard, and so (for his two-year tenure in Montpellier) was Nicolas-Charles-Gabriel.

Louis-Cyr-Charlemagne, the third of Jean-Baptiste's sons by Jeanne-Gabrielle Berger, became executioner at Provins; his house, known as La Maison du Bourreau is still standing, in a narrow lane called the Allée du Bourreau at the lower end of the town outside the ramparts. He subsequently took over Charles-Henri's duties at Versailles, and it was Louis-Cyr-Charlemagne who received the first guillotine allotted to the département of Seine-et-Oise. His son, Louis-Henri Gabriel, turned his back on the family profession and learned the locksmith's trade, only to discover that despite his skill he was unable to earn a living. Because of the Sanson name, no one would patronize his shop.

Jean-Baptiste's daughter, Marie-Josephe, married her first cousin Jean-Louis, the executioner of Reims. There were three more sons, Pierre-Charles, Jean-Baptiste-Pierre, and Joseph-Claude, and lastly a daughter, Gabrielle, about whom nothing is known.

The family led a well-ordered life, the children learning to read and to write, and the entire family attending High Mass on Sundays. Jean-Baptiste himself arose at dawn each day and went to mass at Saint-Laurent like any good bourgeois. On days when he had no executions to perform, he saw his patients and attended to their needs, stopping at one o'clock for his midday meal. In the afternoon he worked in his garden for an hour, then retired to his small laboratory where he studied the physical and natural sciences, with particular emphasis on botany. So effective were the salves and unguents he concocted of roots and herbs that the formulae were used by all of his descendants. Before dinner he'd sit on his doorstep and exchange gossip with his neighbors, all of whom knew him for a kind, charitable man whom they not only respected but liked.

One day the comte de Charolais, one of the sons of the prince de Condé, brought his armorer and engraver—a man named Chesnau—to see Jean-Baptiste. A gun the man had been repairing had exploded, crushing his chest, breaking his wrist, and lacerating both cheeks. Jean-Baptiste's knowledge of anatomy and skill in setting bones, combined with the medications he himself had invented, cured the armorer in two months—an achievement so pleasing to the comte that he spread the story in royal circles. Jean-Baptiste's clientele increased substantially, not only in numbers, but in wealth and social position, enabling him to charge high fees to the rich and to treat the poor for nothing. More like his grandfather Charles than either of his parents, Jean-Baptiste enjoyed the reputation of being a humanitarian—an extraordinary feat for an executioner.

In 1754, at the age of thirty-five, he suffered a stroke that left his right side paralyzed. (Not inconceivably, this misfortune may have been caused by the tension of his existence, the effort of trying to control his emotions and choke back an innate disgust for his hated profession.) He retired to the little farmhouse at Brie-Comte-Robert, about twenty miles from Paris, which his grandfather had purchased in 1703. The house is still standing near what is now the Route Nationale 19, which runs from Paris through Brie-Comte-Robert to Provins and Troyes and on into Switzerland.

The quiet of the countryside, the slow untroubled existence, and—probably more than anything—the cessation of dread and fear succeeded in effecting a cure. In 1761 Jean-Baptiste, in need of work, asked for and received the title of executioner for the bailliwick of Brie-Comte-Robert. In 1766, having regained the complete use of his limbs, he and his wife returned to Paris.

Meanwhile, however, there was need for an executioner in the capital city. As soon as word got about that Jean-Baptiste could no longer perform his duties, executioners from provincial towns hastened to Paris, hopeful of securing the coveted position. But they had not reckoned with Marthe Dubut. Taking her grandson, the fifteen-year-old Charles-Henri, by the hand, the indomitable woman marched him to the office of the Public Prosecutor, only to discover that she was not the first to arrive. Two competitors from the provinces already had reached the official and offered 24,000 livres for the post. These two men, a father and son, had no sooner emerged from the Prosecutor's presence when she threatened them: they must leave Paris immediately or she would see that they went to prison—an idle threat perhaps, but tales of the Sanson influence and the Sanson power had been circulating for years. Intimidated by this knowledge, the would-be executioners fled from her like a pair of guilty felons.

She won the appointment for Charles-Henri. Parlement decreed that he should replace his father, thereby guaranteeing the succession, although even the Parlement of Paris could not invest him legally until Jean-Baptiste's death.

Charles-Henri Sanson has been called La
Clef de Voûte de la Révolution, the keystone of the
Revolution. Durig the bloodstained years that began in
1789, he was known variously as Maître Sanson, Le
Grand Sanson, Charlot (a nickname bestowed upon him
because of his christian name, which was also that of
most members of his family), and Sans-Farine. This last
is an elaborate pun, based on the fact that the executioner used bran sacks, or *sacs de son*, to hold the heads of
his guillotined victims. His sacks would then be *sans son*,
without bran, a phrase identical in pronunciation to
Sanson's name and providing an easy transposition to the
more generic Sans-Farine, without grain.

Born on February 15, 1739, he was sent away from
home at an early age in an attempt to remove him from
the parish where his family's name and profession were
known, an attempt at anonymity which failed in his case
as it would fail with succeeding generations of Sansons.
The moment his classmates discovered his identity, life
became intolerable and his parents were compelled to
remove him from the school in Rouen and bring him
back to Paris. They sent him to the *pension* of a Sieur
Hardy, but he had to leave there for the same reason.
Realizing that the only solution to their problem was
private tutoring, Jean-Baptiste engaged the services of
the Abbé Grisel, a parish priest who agreed to come to
the house in the rue Poissonnière and take charge of
Charles-Henri's education. The boy was apparently of

average intelligence but not a very good student, absorbing more of the Abbé's religious and moral principles than he did of academic fact.

From the age of eleven, he acted as assistant to his father, but his appearances on the scaffold were infrequent. In January 1754 Jean-Baptiste retired, and although Charles-Henri had not been formally invested with the title, he was nevertheless executioner of Paris and had to be present on the scaffold. In January 1755, the sixteen-year-old lad officiated for the first time. A man named Ruxton was to be broken on the wheel. Following in the footsteps of his great-grandfather, the boy merely assisted, letting his aides do the work. And like grand-père Charles he acquitted himself shamefully, recoiling and turning his head from the horrible sight.

Shortly thereafter, a man called Mongeot was to be bludgeoned and then subjected to the wheel for having killed the husband of his mistress, Madame Lescombat. Snow was falling that day, and trembling with cold and dread, Charles-Henri stood on the scaffold, as far as possible from the mulatto who was doing the bludgeoning. While poor Mongeot was stretched on the wheel (it took him two hours to die), Madame Lescombat was brought to the scene by an armed guard and made to witness her lover's agony. (Guilty of having incited Mongeot to the murder, the lady would later be hanged.) She was a celebrated beauty and the sight of her anguish doubled Charles-Henri's abhorrence and disgust.

Old Marthe Dubut, present at the scaffold to make sure that her grandson performed his job properly, shouted at him throughout the execution, alternating her cries of encouragement with sharp reprimands, highly displeased and angry with the frightened boy for having averted his eyes.

[40]

Madame Lescombat claimed to be pregnant, hence the delay in her own execution. If a woman declared herself pregnant, she would be imprisoned for two months, during which time the veracity of her claim could be proved or disproved. If she were indeed pregnant, she was permitted to have the child; if not, she would be hanged as soon as the falsity of her claim had been ascertained. Two months after the death of Mongeot, Charles-Henri was ordered to hang her. A contemporary account reports that "a vast crowd gathered in the place de Grève and in the streets adjacent to it, to witness her passage. The crowd stretched back as far as the towers of Notre Dame. . . . When she climbed to the scaffold people clapped as if they were at the theater. And during the execution, street vendors sold sketches of the victim along with pamphlets relating the story of her crime."

No less horrified by the blood-lust of the populace than by the barbarity and cruelty of his own task, Charles-Henri's initial experiences would soon pale by comparison with a task still to come. On January 5, 1757, Robert-François Damiens attempted to assassinate Louis XV. Due to the fact that the King was wearing two fur coats, the knife didn't penetrate very deeply, but whether attempted or accomplished, regicide was a serious crime. Damiens was tried, convicted, and sentenced to death by the Parlement of Paris, the words of the decree so brutal as to be almost unbelievable:

> The Court declares Robert-François Damiens duly convicted of the crime of Lèse-majesté, divine and human, for the very wicked, very abominable and very detestable parricide perpetrated on the King's person: and therefore condemns the said Damiens to *amende honorable*

before the principal church of Paris, whither he shall be taken in a cart wearing only a shirt and holding a taper of the weight of two pounds; and then, on his knees, he shall say and declare that, wickedly and with premeditation, he has perpetrated the said very wicked, very abominable and very detestable parricide, and wounded the King with a knife in the right side, for which he repents and begs pardon of God, the King and Justice; and further the court orders that he then be taken to the Grève, and, on a scaffold erected for the purpose, that his chest, arms, thighs and calves be burnt with pincers; his right hand, holding the knife with which he committed the said parricide, burnt in sulfur; that boiling oil, melted lead, and rosin and wax mixed with sulfur be poured into his wounds; and after that his body be pulled and dismembered by four horses, and the members and body consumed in fire, and the ashes scattered to the winds. The court orders that his property be confiscated to the King's profit; that before the said execution Damiens be subjected to the *question ordinaire et extraordinaire* to make him confess the names of his accomplices. Orders that the house in which he was born be demolished, and that no other building be erected on that spot.

Decreed by the Parlement on March 26, 1757.

Charles-Henri was appalled. No man had been quartered in France since François Ravaillac, the assassin of Henri IV, and that had taken place in 1610, over a century earlier. The mere reading of his orders sent shivers down the executioner's back, and the thought of having to carry them out filled him with such disgust and

[42]

revulsion that he knew he'd never be able to do it. He wanted to see his father, but Jean-Baptiste and Madeleine were still living in Brie-Comte-Robert, too far away for the eighteen-year-old boy to reach him. He had no recourse except to go to his grandmother and confess that he was not equal to the task.

The shrewd old woman realized that Charles-Henri was telling the truth. His suggestion that he resign was out of the question. If she forced him to carry out Damiens' punishment, he'd disgrace not only himself but the entire Sanson family. The only solution was to summon her son Gabriel, Jean-Baptiste's brother, the executioner of Reims. Charles-Henri would be obliged to legalize the proceedings by his presence, but he could serve as his uncle's assistant. Charles-Henri accepted this reprieve gratefully. For Marthe Dubut, the occasion would be the triumph of her life; there would be not one but two Sansons on the scaffold!

As executioner of Reims, Gabriel really had no right to officiate in Paris; but as "Exécuteur des sentences et jugements de l'Hôtel du Roi et Grande Prévôté de France," his presence on the scaffold was quite legal. This title was purely honorary, as there had been no sentences handed down by the Provost Marshal of the royal household since the days of Louis XI. But the job still existed and paid 3,300 livres a year.

The first step in organizing the execution consisted of searching for and purchasing four strong horses. For these, Gabriel had to pay 432 livres. Secondly, and far more difficult, a man had to be hired to administer the torture ordered by Parlement, because neither Gabriel nor any of the assistants wanted any part of the procedure. By an odd coincidence, the old fellow who consented to carry out the preliminary torture was named Soubise—the grandson of the man who had executed Ravaillac.

At five o'clock on the morning of March 28, Gabriel and Charles-Henri dressed in their official costume and got into their cart. They were followed by the four horses and by fifteen assistants. At the Conciergerie prison they witnessed the *question*, or torture inflicted on the victim before death, which was supposed to make him reveal his accomplices. Despite having his arms dislocated by *l'estrapade* and his feet twisted by the torturous "boot," Damiens revealed nothing, because he had nothing to reveal. The man was a religious fanatic, acting on his own. His body was wrapped in a sack from which only his head remained free. Then he was taken to the Sainte-Chapelle, where he was placed on a wooden bench. There he lay for several hours, listening to the lengthy sermon of the almoner.

Not until mid-afternoon was the poor man taken to the place de Grève where Soubise waited for him on the scaffold. By this time, the torturer had managed to get himself so drunk that he could barely stand up. Regretting his decision to do the job, he had tried to bolster his courage with wine, and in the process had forgotten to buy the wax, lead, oil, and sulfur specified in his orders. Gabriel cursed him, only to be cursed in turn by the Public Prosecutor, while the crowd roared with laughter at Soubise's drunken antics. After a great deal of confusion, two assistants were sent to buy the necessary materials and Damiens was finally brought forward and pulled from his sack.

A quaking Gabriel managed to deafen himself to his victim's shrieks and hold the man's right hand to a flaming brazier; minutes later one of the assistants applied red-hot pincers to Damiens' already mutilated body while another poured boiling oil and lead into the wounds. The quartering was a nightmare. Three times Damiens' limbs were attached to the horses and the executioner's aides whipped the beasts, and three times they started off, dislocating the limbs but failing to separate them from the trunk of his body. An axe was finally needed to complete the odious task.

Almost as loathsome as the execution itself was the blood-lust of a tumultuous crowd. The ubiquitous Barbier recorded the event in his *Journal*: "Every rooftop in the vicinity of the place de Grève was covered with people. And one could not help but remark on how many women were present, women of distinction. They seemed to weather the horrors of the execution even better than the men, which fact does not exactly do them honor."

Another man who both witnessed and recorded the event is considered somewhat more of an expert on the subject of women than Barbier. Casanova's *Mémoires* devote several paragraphs to that memorable afternoon, during which he, in company with a male companion and three ladies, watched it from a window overlooking the place de Grève.

> We watched the horrible spectacle for four hours, [reports Casanova]. During the death of this victim of the jesuits, I was compelled to turn my head from the sight and to stop up my ears when I heard his anguished cries . . . but la Lambertini and the old aunt [two of the ladies present] made not the slightest movement; is this not proof of their hard-heartedness? I had to pretend to believe them when they told me that the horror of this monster's deed was greater than any sense of pity they could feel for his torment.

[45]

Casanova's concern for Damiens did not prevent him from observing a more frivolous little drama that occurred during the execution:

> The fact is that Tiretta [the other man] kept the pious aunt singularly occupied throughout the execution: and perhaps that is the reason why this virtuous lady dared not move nor even turn her head.
>
> Finding himself directly behind her [at the window] he [Tiretta] had taken the precaution of turning back the skirt of her dress so that he would not step on it. . . . I [Casanova] heard rustling during a two-hour period and finding the situation most amusing, I forced myself not to move during all that time. I marveled at my own desire even more than I admired the boldness of Tiretta; but most of all I admired the amazing sang-froid of the pious aunt.
>
> When, at the end of this long period I saw Madame *** turn around, I turned too, and gazed at Tiretta; he looked as cool, as insouciant, as collected as if nothing had happened, but the dear old aunt seemed a bit more pensive and grave than usual. She had found herself in the awkward position of having to close her eyes to what was happening, of having to ignore it, lest she cause la Lambertini to laugh at her, and lest she horrify her young niece in revealing to her mysteries about which she should know nothing.

Gabriel Sanson never recovered from the events of that afternoon; returning to Reims, he abdicated his position in favor of his son, ceding his honorary title to his nephew in return for a pension of 2,400 livres. With Jean-Baptiste

[46]

living in the country and Gabriel in retirement, Charles-Henri at the age of eighteen now reigned supreme as the one and only *Bourreau de Paris.*

The execution of Damiens signaled the real beginning of Charles-Henri's career in that it forced him to recognize and to accept the terrible and the inevitable. It was a grave, a more mature Charles-Henri who now shouldered the responsibilities of his office, and there were logical reasons for the change in his character. First of all, the very youth that made him impressionable also allowed him to forget what was past. Secondly, his guilt was mitigated in his own mind because he had not actually taken part in the execution but had merely been a witness to it. Thirdly and most importantly, he lived under the same roof as Marthe Dubut and the drumbeat of her principles and her prideful assertions pounded in his ears without pause: The position of the executioner is an honorable one, his mission in life is important; his task may be difficult, even painful at times, but his job is as vital to the maintenance of law and order in the kingdom as that of any soldier or policeman. He has every right to hold his head high. The redoubtable Marthe was taking no chances on the Sanson heritage, it must go on.

Like Sanson de Longval, Charles-Henri was a tall, strong man, with classic features and a pleasant manner. In his *quartier* he enjoyed the reputation of being a respected neighbor who was charitable and kind to the poor. Basically serious, he preferred solitude to society and avoided public places, shunned social gatherings. A creditable musician, he played both the violin and the cello. He found solace in music, especially after an execution.

Another trait inherited from his Abbeville ancestor did not prove as advantageous as his good looks: snobbery was not the right of a headsman, and Charles-Henri was a snob. Not only did he call himself the chevalier de Longval, but he wore blue coats and carried a sword, affectations that soon got him into trouble. Both the weapon and the color belonged to the aristocracy; blue being the alleged color of noble blood (hence the expression blue-blood), those of low rank were forbidden to wear it. Summoned to appear before the Public Prosecutor, Charles-Henri was given a stern reminder that he, Sanson, an executioner, and thus a person of extremely low station, had no right to dress in this fashion, that he had committed a serious offense, and that the situation must be remedied immediately. Infuriated but undaunted, Charles-Henri adopted green as his color and ordered his coats cut in a new and distinctive way, which caught the eye of the marquis de Letorières, one of the Versailles coterie. The marquis not only admired Charles-Henri's style but copied it, with the result that it became fashionable to dress "à la Sanson"— no small triumph for the self-styled chevalier de Longval.

At the zenith of its power and privilege during the first half of the eighteenth century, the nobility enjoyed numerous and varied prerogatives, among them the rights of the hunt. Strangely enough, the Sanson family had always enjoyed this privilege, based possibly on their claim to the seigneurie de Longval, but more probably because they had never been found hunting in the same place or at the same time as persons of noble rank. Charles-Henri was genuinely fond of the sport, a fondness of upper-class privilege that would once again involve him in difficulties.

One evening on his way home from a foray into the countryside, he stopped at an inn. He entered the dining room, and because he cut rather a striking figure, he was asked by a young noblewoman if he would join her for dinner. When she asked him his name, he replied: "I am the chevalier de Longval, an officer of the Parlement." After dinner, the young marquise accepted his offer to escort her to her rooms. He hesitated outside her door, realizing that she wanted him to spend the night with her, and would have succumbed to her charms but for the fact that he had to be back in Paris early the next morning to prepare for an execution. He departed abruptly. Furious at the rebuff, she waited until she heard the sound of his horse's hoofs clattering away from the courtyard of the inn, then went downstairs and asked if anyone knew the young man's identity. As luck would have it, one of the other guests had recognized him, and quickly disabused her of the idea that she had dined with an aristocrat. "Why he's the *Bourreau* of Paris, Madame" said her informant with a laugh. "I've seen him on the place de Grève many times."

Returning to Paris, she lost no time in consulting a lawyer, demanding that Charles-Henri be made to appear in court to offer a public apology to her for the offense of having dined with her. In addition, she asked that all executioners be made to wear some distinctive mark on their clothing so that everyone would know who they were and could avoid contact with them.

Charles-Henri could get no lawyer to defend him. No man of honor would touch the case, so the executioner acted in his own defense, his words echoing the oft-repeated phrases of his indomitable grandmother. He argued the importance of the executioner as an officer of the law; he stated that he killed men in the same way and for the same reasons as any soldier—to protect the

[49]

kingdom and to protect his fellow men; that his job was as respectable and his station in life as honorable as any other.

"Ask any soldier what his profession entails," said the executioner proudly. "He will answer as I do, that he kills men. No one flees his company for that reason; no one refuses to eat with him. Who does he kill? Innocent people, people who are serving their country just as he is. I too serve my country, but I respect innocence. I kill only the guilty."

The eloquence of his plea must have impressed the court, because the case was dismissed.

Not long after this episode, an old friend reentered the life of the Sansons. Frère Ange Gomard, Abbé de Picpus had been a patient of Jean-Baptiste's, but the entire family had known him and now they welcomed him heartily. Before long he became a regular guest at the Sanson dinner table, and during the course of conversation they learned that he had a niece of whom he was very fond. Unfortunately the girl, Jeanne Bécu Gomard de Vaubernier by name, was also a source of worry. Brought up by the sisters of the Sacré Coeur convent, Jeanne afterward had become companion to the widow of a *fermier-général*, a kind of tax collector, and made the mistake of falling into bed with the widow's oldest son. She then took up with the second son, compounding the felony. Dismissed in disgrace, she found work with a dressmaker in the rue St. Honoré, where her beauty and charm were noticed by the husbands of many clients. At present she was the mistress of a certain Jean du Barry who had promised to marry her but seemed in no rush to formalize their relationship. Charles-Henri was intrigued by the Abbé's description of this beautiful and charming woman, promised to go to see her, allegedly to persuade

[50]

her to mend her ways, but actually in the hope of receiving her favors.

It has been said that Charles-Henri and the future Madame du Barry, mistress of Louis XV, had a love affair. But the probability is slim, inasmuch as the lady had far greater ambitions and far more interesting and profitable opportunities for advancement than could be offered by the executioner of Paris. But Charles-Henri did see her more than once during the years preceding his marriage; twenty-seven years later it would be his painful duty to escort her from the Conciergerie to the scaffold, there to watch his son direct her execution.

Charles-Henri's introduction to his future bride was the direct result of his passion for hunting. In order to reach the wooded region outside the village of Montmartre, which abounded in game, he had to pass the establishment of Jacques Jugier, a market-gardener in the village, and it soon became his habit to stop and have a glass of wine with the gardener and his family. The prospect of marriage with his eldest daughter Marie-Anne undoubtedly appealed to Charles-Henri, not only because she was a good housekeeper and a pious woman, but because, being a snob, he did not relish the thought of linking himself with the daughter or sister of an executioner, and his choice outside his profession was not a large one. The Jugiers were poor but respected, and Marie-Anne, although six years older than her bridegroom, would make him a loyal and devoted wife.

On January 20, 1766, Charles-Henri Sanson married her. The bridegroom's witnesses were Charles-Jean-Baptiste Sanson, father of the bridegroom, and Nicolas-Charles-Gabriel Sanson, his uncle. Those of the bride were Joseph Robin, a wine merchant residing in the rue Montmartre, parish of Saint-Eustache, and Martin Séguin, fireworks-maker for the Revels of the King, resident in the rue Dauphine, parish of Saint-Sulpice. They would have two sons—Henri, born in 1767, who succeeded his father as executioner, and Gabriel, born two years later, who died tragically in a fall from the revolutionary scaffold.

The ménage of the Sanson family resembled that of any Parisian bourgeois of the period. It was an unwritten law that no reference be made to Charles-Henri's profession, with the result that even visitors thought themselves in the house of an ordinary, respectable, solid citizen—which was in fact, the truth. Marie-Anne was an exemplary wife and an excellent mother. Being a religious woman, she conducted prayers morning and evening for the family and for the executioner's assistants, who were part of the household and always served at table. At least twice a year while old Marthe Dubut was alive, the entire family gathered around the dining table in the faubourg Poissonnière; and at those times, the servants always addressed the Sanson men as Monsieur de Provins, Monsieur de Blois, Monsieur de Reims, never by their given names. Twenty-five or thirty people assembled for these dinners, Marthe naturally presiding at the head of the table. When he came to Paris, Jean-Baptiste would sit opposite her in his wheelchair; between them sat the younger members of the family, and occasionally invited guests. The Sansons rarely went out, feeling more at ease in their own house among their own kind. This pattern of existence would grow more rigid during the revolutionary years when Charles-Henri's profession necessitated building a protective wall around his private life.

On May 9, 1766, comte Lally Tollendal came back

into the lives of the Sansons—not as a young lieutenant seeking shelter from the rain as he had done during the wedding festivities of Jean-Baptiste, but as a *maréchal* of France who had been sentenced to death. When war broke out with England in 1756, he had been given the command of a French expedition to India. A courageous man and a capable general, he had fought gallantly for France, but his pride and his arrogance had grown with the years. He was disliked by his troops and hated by the natives, whom he regarded as slaves. Everything went wrong for him, and after a series of defeats, he was forced to surrender, thereby losing India to the English. While a prisoner of war in England, he learned that his own country had accused him of treachery and that the King demanded his head. Against all advice, he returned to Paris to stand trial. Logic told him that as a soldier, he would be judged by the military; pride deluded him into the belief that he could exonerate himself. He miscalculated on both counts; not only was he thrown into the Bastille and made to wait two years for a trial, but a civil court condemned him for betraying the interests of the King and sentenced him to death.

As soon as he learned of the sentence, Jean-Baptiste remembered his promise to the young lieutenant and returned to Paris. Although by this time he had recovered the use of his limbs, Charles-Henri's father realized that he wouldn't have the strength to wield the heavy sword used to execute members of the nobility. His son must keep the promise for him.

Both Sansons accompanied the sixty-four-year-old Lally Tollendal from the Bastille to the place de Grève. It is said that the condemned man, recognizing Jean-Baptiste, asked him to remember and to honor his promise. The executioner, whose muscles had long since atrophied, could only cast an apologetic glance at Lally Tollendal and indicate that his son must act for him.

Unfortunately for the victim, Charles-Henri had never before used the heavy sword. Unfortunately, too, at the instant that his blade came down upon Lally's neck, the prisoner's long white hair loosed itself from the cord that held it, and the blade slipped, managing only to break the man's jaw. The crowd burst into shouts of anger, the executioner's assistants sprang forward to hold Lally who was writhing on the ground, while Charles-Henri stood motionless, too frightened to lift his bloodied sword a second time. Suddenly, and with a fierce strength that must have surprised him as much as it did the onlookers, Jean-Baptiste grabbed the sword from his son's hand and, raising it above his head, brought it down upon comte Lally's neck, severing his head with one blow. Almost immediately, his emotions as spent as his body, the retired executioner fainted.

An experience such as this left its mark on the entire family; Jean-Baptiste and his wife Madeleine departed for Brie-Comte-Robert, the old executioner vowing never again to leave his country retreat. Marie-Anne tried to comfort her husband as best she could, but her consolation—if indeed she succeeded in comforting him—was destined to be short-lived. Barely a month later, Charles-Henri was called upon to use the sword again, and this time his father would not be present to come to his assistance.

The chevalier de la Barre, aged nineteen, had been sentenced to be decapitated and then burned for the crime of sacrilege, his execution to take place in Abbeville. Under ordinary circumstances, this task would not have fallen to Charles-Henri, but the executioner of

Abbeville had been taken ill. Although there were executioners in Amiens and in Rouen, "Monsieur de Paris" received orders to perform the decapitation. Remembering that his ancestors came from Abbeville must have made his journey doubly trying, but this time Charles-Henri carried out his orders surely, swiftly, and neatly. It is interesting to note, however, that in Henri Sanson's *Memoirs*, in the chapter on the chevalier de la Barre, he quotes Charles-Henri as saying: "The executioner who exercises his profession because he likes it, and who admires his own talents of destruction, is an absurd fiction."

On July 30, 1778, knowing himself near death, Jean-Baptiste obtained permission from the King to resign his post so that his son might accede to the title; and in August of the same year, Charles-Henri received his *lettre de provision*, the document confirming his appointment. In return for it, he paid the sum of six thousand livres to the Royal Treasury.

After his father's death, Charles-Henri sold the house in the rue Poissonnière, sharing the proceeds with his brothers and sisters. Less than one hundred years earlier that house and the land around it had cost Charles Sanson six thousand livres. His great-grandson sold the property for one hundred thousand. Charles-Henri then rented a house at number ten rue Neuve Saint-Jean. Although smaller than the previous dwelling, it had ample living space for his family and his assistants, a large garden, and outbuildings for his horses, carriages, and the tools of his trade. He kept the farm at Brie-Comte-Robert, where both he and his wife enjoyed planting flowers and vegetables, pruning trees, and walking through the countryside. He was now thirty-nine years old and Marie-Anne forty-five; their two sons were robust lads. The older one, Henri, had already been present on the scaffold at age eleven.

During the next eight years, such executions as occurred did not involve members of the nobility, which meant that Charles-Henri needed only to preside, letting his aides do the work. Not until 1786 was his active participation required. That event, which shook France to its foundations and contributed in no small part to the coming Revolution, involved him in the punishment of Jeanne de la Motte Valois. The story is better known as the Affair of the Diamond Necklace.

The famous necklace originally had been ordered by Louis XV as a gift for Madame du Barry, but when he died prior to its completion, he had left the court jewelers Charles Boehmer and Paul Bassenge with an object in their possession that they could not sell. Consisting of 647 diamonds at a total weight of 2,800 carats, it was priced at 1,800,000 livres, too high even for the extravagant Marie Antoinette.

Jeanne de la Motte Valois was a young woman who claimed descent from Henri II by his mistress Nicole de Savigny. In 1780 Jeanne married comte Antoine de la Motte, an impecunious army officer whose expectations failed to match her hopes. Being both beautiful and charming, she had no difficulty in finding a lover more to her liking. Louis-René-Edouard de Rohan, Prince-Archbishop of Strasbourg and Grand Almoner of France, belonged to a family whose position, power, and wealth were unrivaled in France. Cardinal de Rohan, however, had made one grievous mistake; when Marie Antoinette had come to France as a young bride, many Frenchmen were hostile to Austria and to *l'Autrichienne*, the little Austrian who had married their King. Rohan had been part of that faction and his dislike of the Queen was no secret. He had expressed his sentiments both in France and subsequently as French ambassador to the Court of Vienna. Now, ten years after the royal marriage, he regretted his words: Marie Antoinette's antipathy for him was preventing him from attaining the one post he coveted, that of Prime Minister.

Aware of Rohan's desire for power and her own for money, Jeanne de la Motte saw what seemed to be a simple method of obtaining both. She managed to convince the Cardinal that she was an intimate of the Queen, that she had spoken of him to the Queen in glowing terms, and that a letter of apology written in his own hand would surely bring royal forgiveness. Blinded by ambition and encouraged in his blindness by the villainous comte Cagliostro, who had great influence on him (and whose help Jeanne had enlisted), Rohan wrote to Marie Antoinette and entrusted the note to Jeanne who promised to deliver it for him.

Jeanne hired a man named Marc-Antoine Rétaux de Villette to imitate Marie Antoinette's handwriting, and a few days after she had allegedly delivered Rohan's apology, she brought him a reply. Composed by Jeanne and forged by Villette, the note, penned on gilt-edged notepaper, informed the Cardinal that his Queen no longer considered him guilty of misconduct and that although an immediate audience was impossible, she would let him know as soon as it could be arranged.

Thus began an exchange of letters, the Queen's (composed by Jeanne) worded so as gradually to increase the Cardinal's confidence that he would be restored to favor. But months passed, Rohan began to express dissatisfaction and then anxiety; Marie Antoinette's words were warm, cordial, but her actions denied them. Why had she not recognized him before the Court?

[57]

Jeanne de la Motte then organized what would be known as the Grove of Venus impersonation. She told the Cardinal that although Marie Antoinette could not yet acknowledge him in public, she would grant him a private interview—at midnight, in the park of Versailles. Rohan, like the rest of the Court, knew that the Queen liked to walk in the park on warm summer evenings, and was rumored to meet her lovers on garden paths and in secluded arbors. One of her favorite spots was known as the Queen's grove, *le bosquet de la Reine*, also called the Grove of Venus because it contained a marble statue of the goddess. Marie Antoinette's fondness for play acting and masquerades was also a known fact, so that a midnight rendezvous seemed quite in character. Rohan had no reason to suspect that his long-awaited audience with the Queen would be nothing more than a farce.

Jeanne had only one problem; she must find someone to impersonate Marie Antoinette, someone whose profile resembled that of the Queen. Her choice fell upon a mademoiselle d'Oliva; and having persuaded the beautiful young girl that she would be rendering a service to her Queen, Jeanne handed her a letter, telling her she must deliver it to a distinguished nobleman, whom she would meet at midnight in the Grove of Venus, just below the Great Terrace of the château. Mademoiselle d'Oliva was to present the letter and a rose to the nobleman when he entered the grove, and to speak the words: "You know what this means."

The rendezvous took place and the Cardinal was overjoyed. He not only believed that he had seen the Queen, but that her words were an indication of future favors—amorous as well as political. He was prepared to execute any commission that might be asked of him; the stage was now set for the Affair of the Diamond

Necklace. The exchange of letters was resumed, and he was persuaded that the Queen desired the necklace, but that because it must be purchased without the King's knowledge, she would pay for it out of her own purse. As proof of her trust in Rohan, he was to arrange the transaction. One of Villette's forgeries duly authorized him to buy the necklace.

Highly flattered and pleased that such an important commission had been entrusted to him, Rohan showed the note to the jewelers, Boehmer and Bassenge. Having no reason to believe themselves the victims of a fraud, they gave the necklace to the Cardinal in return for his promise that it would be paid for in installments. The Abbé Georgel, Rohan's secretary and vicar-general, continues the story in his *Memoirs*, quoted by Frances Mossiker in *The Queen's Necklace*:

> Madame de la Motte, intoxicated with joy at the fantastic success of her fantastic intrigue, had set the stage at her Versailles apartment for the grand finale, the transfer of the diamond necklace into the hands of the man who would present himself as the emissary of the Queen. Here were, in very truth, a stage and a performance.
>
> The Cardinal, at the appointed hour of twilight on the appointed day, February 1, made his way to Madame de la Motte's, followed by his personal valet with the jewel case. This man the Cardinal dismissed at the door; then, taking the great leather case into his own hands, he went in alone. Here was the sacrificial victim, ready to be offered up on the altar of his own good faith.
>
> The stage consisted of a room with a small alcove, a glass-paneled door serving as divider. The talented playwright of the comedy ushered

[59]

the spectator to a seat in the alcove.

As the curtain rises, the stage is in semidarkness; one small lamp provides the only light. A door opens and a voice rings out:

"In the name of the Queen!"

Madame de la Motte advances respectfully, picks up the jewel case and hands it to the self-announced messenger of Her Majesty.

Thus was the transfer of the diamond necklace effected.

The Prince, the silent and concealed spectator, believed he had recognized the messenger; Madame de la Motte said it was the Queen's confidential valet from Trianon—the same one the Prince had observed escorting Madame de la Motte out of the palace gates one moonlit night. There was a similarity of stature, and both had worn the livery of the Queen.

The Cardinal felt complete assurance that the necklace had reached its proper destination.

The Abbé Georgel claims that some stones from the necklace were kept for personal use by Madame de la Motte and Villette, but that most were taken to London by Monsieur de la Motte. They were then sold, and the money used to maintain Madame de la Motte in a style befitting a descendant of the Valois.

When Rohan paid only part of the price instead of the full installment he had promised, the jewelers submitted their bill to the Queen. She quite honestly denied having ordered the necklace, either verbally or in writing. When the matter reached King Louis XVI, he immediately recognized the notes as forgeries. Aware of the Cardinal's sentiments toward his wife, he concluded that the plot had been concocted to discredit the Queen. Rohan was sent to the Bastille and implicated Jeanne, who in turn revealed the names of all the others concerned. All were put in prison and later tried in open court.

Marie Antoinette attempted to persuade officials that although Rohan had been innocent of complicity in the fraud, his conduct had been an affront to her honor and position, that he had committed the crime of lèse-majesté. He was nonetheless declared innocent of all charges. This complete vindication of the Cardinal was a direct attack on the monarchy, and one of the early portents of the oncoming Revolution. Cagliostro and Rétaux de Villette were also set free, but Jeanne de la Motte was sentenced to be whipped, branded on both shoulders with the letter "V" signifying *voleuse* (thief), and imprisoned for life.

Minor punishments such as whipping and branding were usually left to the executioner's aides, but because the comtesse de la Motte was of noble blood, her punishment had to be undertaken by the executioner himself.

In an attempt to keep the scandalous affair as quiet as possible, Charles-Henri received orders to execute the punishment in the early hours of the morning, not at the Pilori des Halles—where whippings and brandings usually took place—but in the courtyard of the Palais de Justice. At five o'clock on the morning of June 21, 1786, he conducted his victim to hear her sentence pronounced by the Parlement. (In France, prisoners did not know their fate except in cases of capital punishment.) Haughty and scornful at first, she refused to kneel, as was customary while judgment was pronounced, but when she learned what was in store for her, her composure vanished. She started to scream and thrash about so violently that Charles-Henri and his aides were forced to tie her up before carrying her to the courtyard where the scaffold had been erected. Despite the early hour and the unannounced and unusual locale, a crowd of hundreds had gathered outside the railings of the courtyard. When her bonds were loosed, Jeanne ran to the edge of the scaffold, forcing Charles-Henri's aides to run after her. She spat in their faces, hurled insults at them, and cursed the Queen, the Cardinal, and all the men who had judged her. With much effort she was finally stripped of her clothing and forced down upon her stomach, while Charles-Henri administered the beating.

In *The Queen's Necklace*, Frances Mossiker quotes from the journal of a certain Nicolas Ruault:

> Her whole body was revealed—her superb body, so exquisitely proportioned. At the flash of those white thighs and breasts, the rabble broke the stunned silence with whistles, catcalls, shouted obscenities.
>
> The prisoner slipping from his grasp, the executioner—branding iron in hand—had to follow her as she writhed and rolled across the paving stones of the courtyard to the very foot of the grand staircase . . .
>
> The delicate flesh sizzled under the red-hot iron. A light bluish vapor floated about her loosened hair. At that moment her entire body was seized with a convulsion so violent that the second letter V was applied not on her shoulder but on her breast, her beautiful breast.
>
> Madame de la Motte's tortured body writhed in one last convulsive movement. Somehow she found strength enough to turn and sink her teeth into the executioner's shoulder, through the leather vest to the flesh, bringing blood. Then she fainted.

Charles-Henri was deeply troubled. Not only was this the first whipping he had administered himself, but whipping and branding were punishments usually meted out to prostitutes and hardened convicts, not to ladies of noble blood. And, as is evident in his own description of her, Charles-Henri was as susceptible to Jeanne de la Motte's charm and beauty as the rest of Parisian society. "She was," says he, "a woman of medium height, with a very good figure, a bit on the plump side. Her face was a pretty one, with charming, mobile features. Only if one analyzed her features closely, did one notice that her nose came to a sharp point, that her expressive mouth was overly large, that her eyes were too small. But she had magnificent hair, very white skin and delicately boned arms and legs. She was dressed (the day of execution) in a boudoir gown of brown and white silk covered with little bunches of roses. Her lace bonnet was held back from her face by the abundance of her hair." The executioner, on this occasion, was extraordinarily observant! (Jeanne de la Motte was taken to the prison of La Salpetrière, there to serve a life sentence. She escaped after six months, and died in London in 1791.)

The branding he performed upon Jeanne de la Motte made Charles-Henri more deeply aware of the fact that he, too, was branded, not only by the gallows embroidered on his vest, but by the very title he bore.

The word *bourreau* was an opprobrious term. Literally, it meant executioner or hangman, but it had the added connotation of brute, inhuman wretch, man without feelings, and Charles-Henri neither thought of himself in those terms nor wanted the world to do so. He consulted a lawyer, with a view to having the word suppressed. The magistrate informed him that the word came from the latin *bourrea*, a willow switch used by the lictors of ancient

[63]

Rome to whip adulterers. And, the lawyer added, any man who beats a woman—in this case Jeanne de la Motte—is a *bourreau*. Charles-Henri then appealed to Louis XVI, asking that His Majesty forbid the use of the word, substituting instead "Exécuteur des Jugements Criminels."

He succeeded, and on January 12, 1787, a judgment of the Conseil du Roi decreed an "*Inhibition et défense de designer sous la dénomination de bourreaux, les exécuteurs des arrêts criminels,*" a prohibition and interdiction against designating by the name of *bourreaux* the executors of criminal judgments.

Charles-Henri would later be mocked for what was thought to be a pretentious request, and caricatured as a royalist who hated and had a horror of his job. He was even portrayed as having died of sorrow at having been required to guillotine the King—all of which was undoubtedly true.

By 1788 the rumbling of the approaching Revolution had become audible; the *ancien régime,* with its class divisions and its system of privileges and power for the few had run its course. This stratification of society, a relic of the feudal era, divided the French people into three groups or estates: the clergy, the nobility and the bourgeoisie or third estate. The people were weary, not only of the inequality of classes, but of the inequality of burdens within sections of the same class.

At the top of the social ladder sat Versailles with its Court of over eighteen thousand. Louis XVI ruled by divine right and was therefore subject to no control; the interests of the state determined policy, and Louis was the state. He made laws, he spent treasury money as he chose, he imprisoned his subjects without trial, he censored the press, he levied taxes. The populace might grumble, but it could do nothing about the fact that Marie Antoinette had five hundred servants, that the royal stables contained one thousand nine hundred horses and several hundred carriages (at an annual cost of nearly eight million livres), and that the King's bill for food and drink alone was over a million and a half livres. Graft was the rule, not the exception: ladies-in-waiting, for instance, managed to add about fifty thousand livres apiece to their income by selling candles, which at Versailles could be lighted only once and which, consequently, were barely consumed at all. During the period just preceding the Revolution, the total cost of maintaining Versailles has been estimated at more than thirty-three million livres a year.

Directly beneath the King in rank and power was the clergy, which owned one fifth of the land and exacted tithes on all agricultural products of the kingdom. In addition, the Church was a feudal landlord, and as such, entitled to dues. Most of this money went to bishops and archbishops—younger sons of the nobility as a rule, who resided at Court and lived the life of courtiers, paying little or no attention to their religious duties. The lower clergy, composed of abbés and parish priests, was paid a pittance and barely managed to eke out a living.

The nobility was within itself a complex hierarchy. On top was the *noblesse d'épée,* the Nobility of the Sword, an old military aristocracy whose titles reached far back into history. It took precedence over the *noblesse de robe,* the Nobility of the Robe, whose lineage was neither as ancient nor as distinguished, and whose membership consisted of judges and magistrates belonging to higher tribunals or parlements. The Nobility of the Sword was itself subdivided into a more powerful group of nobles residing at Court and the lesser and considerably poorer families who remained on their country estates.

The third estate with its millions of unprivileged subjects, contained its own divisions. The bourgeoisie separated into an upper middle class consisting of lawyers, doctors, teachers, men of letters, merchants and bankers, and a lower middle class which included the artisans, small shopkeepers and servants.

Below the third estate, on the lowest rung of the ladder, were the peasants, numbering about twenty million.

Because the government was complicated, graft-ridden, and badly administered (and because the Court was given to frivolity and wild extravagance), expenditures always exceeded income—which meant more taxes, most of which were paid by the third estate. There was a tax on real estate and the *taille* (a tax on personal property and income), and the nobility and clergy were exempt from both. To add to the burden, individuals known as *fermiers-généraux* paid a lump sum to the state and could then collect as much money as they desired from bourgeois, artisan, and peasant. But the *gabelle* or salt tax was the one that inflicted the most hardship. Every person over seven years of age was required to buy at least seven pounds of salt a year, whether he wanted it or not. That seven pounds could be used only for cooking or on the table. If a man wanted to salt down and preserve fish or meat, he had to buy an additional amount. It was estimated that thirty thousand people were imprisoned each year and over five hundred condemned to death or sent to the galleys for illegal trade in salt. Wine, assessed at the site of manufacture and again at the time of sale, could also be taxed as many as thirty or forty times as it traveled from its point of origin through the provincial towns to Paris.

Liberty did not exist. Protestantism had been outlawed since the Revocation of the Edict of Nantes in 1685, Jews were considered to be foreigners and treated as second-class citizens, Catholics were required by law to observe communion, fast days, and Lent. Nor did the law permit the formation of societies or the convening of public gatherings. The authorities could arrest and imprison whomever they wished and for as long as they chose. Quite frequently the famous *lettres de cachet* were used to pay off a personal grudge.

And, as if all of these restrictions and hardships did not result in enough suffering, nature provided an additional fillip. The summer of 1788 brought a terrible drought. A violent hailstorm on July thirteenth ruined a large part of the already meager crop, and the harvest was one of the poorest in many years. When the ensuing winter turned so cold that the Seine froze, and nine-tenths of the populace could afford neither firewood nor food, it is small wonder that brigands roved the streets. Tension mounted, grumbling grew louder, and private grievances began to turn to public violence.

Quite logically, Charles-Henri Sanson became the living symbol of official tyranny and injustice. His mere appearance, on the scaffold or anywhere else in Paris, generated an atmosphere of resentment and anger. Equality and justice for all was the cry of the starved populace—and equality of justice, one justice for all. Kill

[67]

a man if needs be, but kill him quickly and mercifully; hang him, cut off his head, but let there be no more quartering or breaking on the wheel. Finally, the people of France had resolved to translate some of their grievances into action, and—but for a miracle—Charles-Henri Sanson might have been one of the first victims.

In August of 1788 he received orders to break a man named Louschart on the wheel. Louschart, a young revolutionary, was imbued with the spirit and the ideas that would result in the storming of the Bastille in less than a year. His father, a widower, was equally fanatic in support of the throne and everything it represented. Both men were articulate and hot-tempered. When the younger man fell in love with a cousin and announced his intention to marry her, his father decided to wed the girl himself to punish his son for his revolutionary ideas. A quarrel ensued, during which the angry father picked up a hammer and threatened his son. Being younger and stronger, Louschart *fils* had no trouble in wresting the instrument away from his sire. Then, not wanting to prolong the fight, he strode toward the door, throwing the hammer back over his shoulder. Unfortunately, his aim proved more accurate than he intended. The hammer struck the older man's forehead, killing him instantly. Murder? Yes, but accidental and unintentional. Death on the wheel was a brutal and unjust sentence.

The populace, getting wind of the circumstances, thronged the place of execution, shouting its anger and threatening Charles-Henri: there should be no execution at all, let alone the inhuman and unjust punishment of the wheel. For the first time in centuries, public feeling exploded. A crowd of men destroyed the scaffold, freed the victim, who was carried off in triumph, and attacked the executioner. Had it not been for the protection of a brawny blacksmith who held off the attackers long enough for Charles-Henri to escape, he would have been trampled to death. Both scaffold and wheel were ripped apart and then burned by the irate mob.

When word of this episode reached the King, he not only pardoned Louschart but ordered that henceforth the penalty of the wheel be abolished in France—a wise decision, and one that found its echo in the courts of justice. Judges suddenly found it prudent to be more lenient in their sentencing and in the type of punishment meted out to criminals. But this newfound humanity came too late to obliterate the memories of past injustice and cruelty, too late to stem a wave of discontent and bitterness that had finally reached its crest. The Revolution had begun.

Only too aware of the unrest, Charles- Henri Sanson interpreted it in terms of his immediate needs. For him, the action of the populace and the subsequent reaction of King and Court had but one result, a lessening of his activity and therefore a decrease in income. And, inasmuch as the Royal Treasury had paid neither his salary nor the small allowance to which he was entitled for traveling expenses, he found himself in desperate financial straits. He had signed promissory notes for food and clothing, for repairs to his carriages, for wine, for feed for his horses, and his creditors were beginning to threaten him with prison. He had no recourse except to petition Louis XVI.

In April of 1789, he was summoned to Versailles. Louis received the executioner in his private apartments. The event is described in the family memoirs:

> The King was standing near a window which opened on the park. Charles-Henri, intimidated by the prestige of royalty, dared advance no further than the threshold, so that the few words they spoke were exchanged at some distance. Louis wore a lilac coat embroidered with gold, short breeches, and pumps; the blue and red ribbons of the order of Saint-Louis hung across his white satin waistcoat. A lace collar and frill was partly covered by a loose cravat which showed the prominent muscles of his neck. The king was of strong but common build. His hair was powdered and curled and was tied with a ribbon at the back of his neck.

The Royal Treasury owed its executioner the sum of 136,000 livres, but as Louis XVI was quick to point out, the Royal Treasury had not sufficient funds with which to pay him. In desperation, Charles-Henri informed His Majesty that an executioner sent to debtor's prison could scarcely carry out the King's justice, and Louis could only agree. But the money was not available. Instead, Charles-Henri was given a *laissez-passer,* a piece of paper:

> "By order of the King
> His Majesty, being desirous of giving
> Monsieur Charles-Henri Sanson the means of

attending to his occupation, has given him a safe-conduct for a period of three months, during which His Majesty orders his creditors to take no proceedings against him; to all solicitors, police officers, or others not to arrest or molest him in any way; to all jailors of prisons not to receive him; and if, in spite of the said prohibition, he be imprisoned, His Majesty orders that he be set free immediately. His Majesty also orders that the present safe-conduct be available only after it has been registered at the office of the Garde du Commerce.

Delivered at Versailles, on the nineteenth of April, seventeen hundred and eighty nine.

Louis.

Unfortunately, although this document forbade Charles-Henri's creditors to demand payment for past debts, it did not order them to extend new credit and thus was of little help to him with current expenses.

The fall of the Bastille on July 14, 1789, signaled the actual beginning of the Revolution, and an exultant population thronged the streets. On July 17th, the King went to the Hôtel de Ville to receive from Jean-Sylvain Bailly, Mayor of Paris, a tri-color *cocarde,* and was cheered by Parisians dreaming of a bright, abundant future. Charles-Henri, who would later guillotine both Louis XVI and Bailly, had no such dreams; the end of absolute monarchy could result only in the end of his means of livelihood—a frightening prospect for a man who knew that a former executioner, no matter how great his skills and abilities, could expect no other employment.

The abolition of capital punishment had become an

important topic; orators in the courtyard of the Palais Royal cried out for it, the newspapers carried daily articles advocating it; and men suddenly recalled the words of Montesquieu who in 1748 wrote in *L'Esprit des lois* that: "Experience has shown that purity and certainty of administration is a more certain deterrent to wrong acts than are cruel punishments." The words and actions of another man were as often quoted, for Voltaire was known and remembered for his spirited defense of Jean Calas and Lally Tollendal, and for his commentary on Cesare Beccaria's essay, *Of Crimes and Punishments*, published in 1766, the year of the execution of the chevalier de la Barre. Voltaire's words on the subject of capital punishment were terse and to the point:

> It is an old saying, [wrote the sage of Ferney,] that a man after he is hanged is good for nothing, and that the punishments invented for the welfare of society should be useful to that society. It is clear that twenty vigorous thieves condemned to hard labor at public works for the rest of their life serve the state by their punishment; and their death would serve only the executioner who is paid for killing men in public. Only rarely are thieves in England punished by death; they are transported overseas to the colonies. The same is true in the vast Russian Empire. Not a single criminal was executed during the reign of the autocratic Elizabeth. Catherine II, who succeeded her, endowed with a very superior mind, followed the same policy. Crimes have not increased as a result of this humanity, and almost always, criminals banished to Siberia become good men. The same has been noticed in the English colonies. This happy change astonishes us, but nothing is more

natural. These condemned men are forced to work constantly in order to live. Opportunities for vice are lacking; they marry and have children. Force men to work and you make them honest. . . . If there really should be one instance in which the law permits a criminal to be put to death who has not committed a capital offense, there will be a thousand instances in which humanity, which is stronger than the law, should spare the life of those whom the law has sentenced to death. . . . The sword of justice is in our hands; but we ought to blunt it more often than sharpen it. It is carried in its sheath before kings to warn us that it should rarely be drawn.

The sword of justice was drawn from its sheath too quickly and too easily in the Paris of 1789, as can be seen from an entry dated October 21st in the diary of Gouverneur Morris, the future American ambassador to France who was in Paris on business at the time:

There has been hanged a baker this morning by the populace, and all Paris is under arms. The poor baker was beheaded according to custom, and carried in triumph through the streets. He had been all night at work for the purpose of supplying the greatest possible quantity of bread this morning. His wife is said to have died of horror when they presented her husband's head stuck on a pole. Surely it is not the usual order of Divine Providence to leave such abominations unpunished. Paris is perhaps as wicked a spot as exists.

A note appended to the entry explains that Denis François, the baker, was innocent of doing anything more than putting aside from the shop supply a few loaves for his family. But someone started the cry that he was hoarding bread.

Charles-Henri realized only too well that certain reforms in the judicial system were necessary, that the public had good cause to cry for Liberté, Égalité, and Fraternité; but he had become desperate in his search for a means to safeguard his job and his income. Concluding that the only way to insure his own position was to perpetuate that of Louis XVI and the monarchy, he permitted a royalist printing press to be installed in his house. (Whether Charles-Henri was—as has been claimed—a sincere advocate of the monarchy is questionable, although he would later show proof of his deep devotion to the royal family as people.) Suddenly Paris was flooded with pamphlets and circulars extolling royalty and denouncing the newborn National Assembly—a state of affairs that could not be permitted to continue. The authorities were quick and efficient; the origin of the scurrilous tracts was discovered, the press confiscated, and the executioner carried off to prison. As might be expected, the newspapers seized upon this story with glee.

The controversy started in the 27th issue of a paper called *Les Révolutions de Paris*, in an article written by its editor, a man named Prud'homme:

> The discovery has just been made that the
> aristocrats now have private printing presses.
> And you will never guess where these presses are
> located . . . at the house of Sanson, *bourreau* of
> Paris! The authorities . . . gained access and

found them all working for the aristocracy. You can imagine, citizens, you can judge by the relationship that has existed between the honest Monsieur Sanson and the aristocrats, what they would gain from his services and talents if they were in power.

The next journalist to join the fray was Gorsas, in his paper, *Le Courrier de Paris et des départements*:

There has been a great deal of talk about the *exécuteur des arrêts criminels* in these last meetings [of the National Assembly, December 24, 1789]. While its members were debating his eligibility or his non-eligibility [for citizenship] he was spending his time trying to become eligible. To wit, he had in his house, printing presses from which emanated all the abominable libel that has been circulated in the provinces to foment revolution and murder. It took place in the ugly and tortuous rue Saint-Jean, in the odious home of the *bourreau*. . . . The presses were confiscated and the honorable *bourreau* was arrested and imprisoned in La Force Prison. . . . It is thought, however, that he will manage to extricate himself . . . he has powerful friends. . . .

L'Espion de Paris et des Provinces informed its readers that Sanson, when questioned by the National Assembly, had defended himself by saying that he had rented his premises in order to earn money for the poor, and knew nothing of the people to whom he had rented them. The *Journal de L'Assemblée Nationale* also reported on his interrogation, and in this version Charles-Henri is al-

[75]

leged to have said he happened to have an empty room in his house and rented it to some workmen who were looking for space. According to this report, he had been taken to the Châtelet prison. But it was Camille Desmoulins in his *Révolutions de France et de Brabant* whose rapier-sharp words found their mark. After subjecting the executioner to a spate of ridicule, he concluded by saying, *J'appelle un chat un chat, et Sanson le bourreau.* (I call a cat a cat, and Sanson the hangman.)

The constant and sarcastic use of the word *bourreau* was not only illegal, having been forbidden by decree of Louis XVI in January of 1787, but insulting and dangerous in the extreme, for it now implied one unworthy of citizenship in the new state. When questioned by the Assembly, Charles-Henri's answers were forceful and proud. He had as much right as anyone in France to hold his head high; fate had bestowed upon him the job of executioner. If his function in life was a cruel one, it was also necessary to law and order. The responsibility for executions belonged more to those who passed sentence than to those who executed it. The sobriquet of *bourreau,* used with such gleeful frequency by the newspapers, intensified and would continue to intensify a prejudice that was as unjust as it was illegal. Once again, Charles-Henri's dignity and pride impressed his listeners, who also chose to believe his statement that he knew nothing of what had been printed and circulated from his house.

The Assembly granted him a conditional release from prison, but the executioner realized that this would not be enough. He consulted Maton de la Varenne, a lawyer, who persuaded him that the best defense would be a good offense and recommended attacking Gorsas. Ordered to appear in court, the journalist failed to answer the summons, with the result that Charles-Henri won his case by default. Gorsas was ordered to retract all of the statements printed in his paper, to pay for the printing and distribution of two hundred copies of the court's verdict, and to pay damages of twenty livres, which money would be given to the poor of the parish of St. Laurent. (At a later date, Desmoulins would also be ordered to pay damages, in his case in the amount of one hundred livres.)

Meanwhile, the Revolution was making progress; fourteen hundred street names were changed in Paris, thereby removing all references to royalty from public view. The place Royale became the place des Fédérés, the place Louis XV was now the place de la Révolution, the rue Bourbon was the rue de Lille, and so forth. In the same manner, reminders of religion and the church were to be erased from the public mind, and so the rues Saint-Denis, Saint-Roch, and Saint-Antoine were short-ened to the rues Denis, Roch, and Antoine; Notre Dame became the Temple de la Raison (The Temple of Reason) and Saint-Gervais the Temple de la Jeunesse (The Temple of Youth). Children were no longer given the names of saints, but revolutionary names such as Brutus, Constitution, Fructidor. The use of the pronoun *tu* (thou) instead of the more formal *vous* was mandatory. The terms of address *monsieur* and *madame* were banished in favor of the more egalitarian *citoyen* and *citoyenne* (citizen and citizeness). All women were obliged by law to wear a cocarde, the tri-color rosette that became a symbol of the Revolution. Punishment for a first offense was eight days in prison; the second time a woman was found without her cocarde, she could be imprisoned for the duration of the Revolution. If in desperation she stripped another woman of her cocarde, the penalty was ten years of solitary confinement.

The Revolution brought changes to the household in the rue Saint-Jean—or rue Jean, as it was now called. And Charles-Henri quickly learned that the new constitutional monarchy was as dilatory in its payments as the old absolute monarchy had been. In addition to a shortage of money, the executioner was faced with an abundance of relatives; two of his brothers had come to Paris to live with him, as had his uncle Gabriel, the retired executioner of Reims, and an ailing sister. There were seventeen mouths to feed: himself, his wife and their two sons, two brothers, his uncle and wife, his sister and eight servants (a cook, four assistants, and three men who drove his carts and looked after his horses). This state of affairs caused the executioner to address an appeal to Roederer, the Public Prosecutor, listing his expenses and imploring him to see that they were paid. This document, entitled *Mémoire instructif pour l'exécuteur des jugements criminels de la Ville de Paris* is dated February 8, 1790. After a preamble in which Charles-Henri reviews the past history of his revenues, and what he had suffered with the suppression of the *droit de havage,* and the inadequate salary of sixteen thousand livres that had been granted in its stead he submits the following list:

EXPENSES OF THE EXECUTIONER

For his two brothers, 600 livres each, so that on days when executions are called for in different localities, they can help him in obeying the orders of the magistrates and perform the said executions	1,200
For four servants, at 300 livres each per year	1,200
For three carters, at 300 livres each per year	900
For one cook, per year	200

For four horses, to be used both city and country	2,000
For the construction of three carriages and one dung-cart	300
Harness and its upkeep	150
Services of the blacksmith, 50 livres per horse per year	200
Mother of the executioner, a pension ordered by the court	1,200
For the food of sixteen people; his wife, his two children, his two brothers, his uncle, aged 75, who has always helped him in performing his duties, an ailing sister, and eight servants at 600 livres	9,600
For the support of his wife, his two children, the extra expenses of the household such as linen, washing, furniture, etc.	4,000
For the rent of his house, containing his family, his servants, his horses, carriages, and the tools of his trade, the said house being located in a place convenient to his place of work	4,800
Taxes per capita, formerly 231 and today	2,048
	27,798

CONTINGENT EXPENSES

Colleagues to help me, when I have need of them, which happens all too often because of the bad character of the servants I am forced to hire, who hold you up for money because they know you must hire them.

Constant tipping, which is a necessity in order to hold those of whom you have need.

Replacement of horses when they die, or the expenses of their sickness.

The illnesses of servants, whom one must keep because one cannot find others to replace them.

The many gifts, which one cannot fail to give.

Expenses on the day of execution.

The tools used for executions, which must be
replaced constantly.

There are a thousand other incidental expenses,
impossible to itemize, because they are of the
moment. All expenses add up to the sum of   5,000

ADDITIONAL OBSERVATIONS

If the executioner is required to take part in the
torturing, or to do any carpentry work, the
following expenses will ensue:

For executing torture, one additional assistant:

For any part of the carpentry work, three
carriages, three horses, harness, the services of a
blacksmith, two carters, two assistant carpenters,
someone to nail the wood together and construct
the scaffold, and lodging for the men, horses,
carriages, and tools; wood to rebuild, upkeep,
extra expenses incurred when I am required to
go out of Paris, replacement of horses . . .   18,000

Charles-Henri was not modest in his estimates but,
having received neither salary nor expenses for some
time, his situation had become desperate. Just how
desperate is evidenced by his final threat: If payment was
not forthcoming, Charles-Henri Sanson would resign as
executioner of Paris.

There is no record of payment, but it must have been
forthcoming, inasmuch as Charles-Henri not only remained in his job but went on to become the "Keystone
of the Revolution."

On August 26, 1789, the Declaration of the Rights of Man proclaimed that men were born free and must remain free and equal before the law. No one could be accused or arrested except where circumstances had been determined by law, and all men would be presumed innocent until proved guilty. On October 9th of the same year Joseph Ignace Guillotin, a deputy to the Constituent Assembly, proposed that the method of execution be the same for all classes of society.

Son of the King's Prosecutor and the ninth of twelve children, Guillotin was born in Saintes, where he received his early education with the Jesuits. He entered a monastery in Bordeaux with the intention of taking orders, but soon abandoned theology for the preliminary degree of Master of Arts, followed by a doctorate in medicine. In 1789 he was not only *docteur-régent* of the Faculty of Medicine in Paris, but one of the most sought-after and most expensive physicians in the capital city. A consultation with him cost as much as thirty-six livres.

In addition to his motion regarding the equality of punishment, Guillotin proposed that henceforth the disgrace of a man's punishment should not extend to his family, that the state should not be permitted to confiscate all of a criminal's worldly goods. The bodies of executed men should be delivered to the family if asked for; if not, they should be buried without mention in the public records of the kind of death they had suffered. Last, but most important, a method of capital punishment must be found that would be both quick and painless.

Guillotin was given the task of finding this method, and plunged into research on the subject. He discovered the mention of a mechanical machine in Holinshed's *Chronicles of Ireland* (1577), the execution by this method allegedly having been performed in 1307. In the memoirs of Jacques Chastenet de Puysegur, the execution at Toulouse in 1632 of the Maréchal Henri II de Montmorency is said to have been performed with neither axe nor sword but a machine. Sir Walter Scott speaks of the "maiden," a form of what would come to be known as a guillotine; and engravings by Albrecht Durer, Lucas Cranach, and others show decapitation by mechanical methods.

Having read up on his subject, Guillotin abandoned the theoretical and sought out the man whose experience and practical knowledge was far greater and consequently far more valuable than any ancient text or engraving—Charles-Henri Sanson. Together they explored and experimented, trying to design a machine which would sever the head from the body quickly and painlessly. In the older methods, the condemned man knelt on the ground, holding his head forward in a position that compelled the blade to descend at an awkward angle, thereby impeding the force of its descent. In their first version, Guillotin and Charles-Henri decided to place the victim flat on the ground. But although this was an improvement on the kneeling position, it proved impractical because after decapitation, the blade undoubtedly would strike the ground and either break or be blunted beyond use.

At their second meeting, Charles-Henri invited his friend and fellow musician Tobias Schmidt to join them. Schmidt, a German maker of clavecins, was a clever mechanic and draughtsman; his design showed a scaffold upon which stood the two grooved uprights of the machine. Between them was the *tranchoir* or blade, which was balanced by a system of lead weights. When the weights were released, the blade plunged rapidly down between the grooves of the uprights. A moveable plank or *bascule* upon which the victim was stretched full-length and tied tightly immobilized his body; and a *lunette* formed by two semi-circular pieces of wood held his head in place. Schmidt estimated that he could build the machine for about 960 livres, but Roederer, the Public Prosecutor, wanted the task entrusted to a master carpenter named Guidon who had had experience in building scaffolds and gallows. Guidon studied the matter and submitted the following estimate:

Timber for the machine, the scaffold, and the staircase leading up to it	1,700	livres
Ironwork	600	
Three *tranchoirs* (two to be held in reserve	300	
Pulleys and the lining of the grooves, in cast copper	300	
Weights of cast iron	300	
Rope	60	
Actual construction, including tests, time spent in the building; and discussion regarding the working of the machine	1,200	
Construction of a working model to be used in demonstrations	1,200	
	5,660	

Guidon's excuse for the exorbitant figure was the difficulty in finding workmen to do the job; most men refused to be associated with the project. He had been able to locate a few men (not in his own employ) who agreed to work for less money, providing they would be exempt from signing the usual working papers, and providing their names would never be made public.

Reasonable or unreasonable as the excuse may have been, Public Prosecutor Roederer was appalled. Schmidt, whose low estimate had probably been the shrewdest tactic of his career, received the contract. The canny maker of clavecins would later be asked to construct thirty-four additional machines for the thirty-four provincial executioners—more business, undoubtedly, than he had ever done in clavecins.

Guillotin's research and the subsequent designs had taken some time to complete, and during these months Charles-Henri Sanson had become the center of attention, associating suddenly with government officials, with deputies to the Assembly, and with physicians. His advice was sought, his ideas considered—and if a lengthy and rather pompous memorandum on the subject of execution is any criterion, Monsieur Sanson's pride and vanity had increased immeasurably.

In June of 1791 the Assembly decreed that henceforth all men condemned to death would have their heads cut off, and that torture was abolished for all time. In March of 1792, Guillotin, Schmidt, and Charles-Henri submitted their finished designs to Antoine Louis, Secretary of the Academy of Surgery, and physician and surgeon to His Most Christian Majesty, Louis XVI. Antoine Louis had his office in the Tuileries Palace, and it was there that he received his visitors. As the four men studied the plans, a door at the back of the room opened and

Charles-Henri Sanson had his second meeting with the King.

Apocryphal or true, the story has been told many times, most dramatically, perhaps, by Alexandre Dumas in *Le Drame de Quatre-Vingt-treize.* "The King," says Dumas, "examined the drawings carefully, and when his eye got to the blade . . . 'the fault is there,' he said, 'the blade should not be crescent-shaped but triangular, and bevelled like a scythe.' And, to illustrate his point, Louis XVI [whose hobby was locksmithery] took a pen in his hand and drew the instrument as he thought it ought to be. Nine months later, the head of the unhappy Louis XVI would be felled by the very instrument he had drawn."

On March 7, 1792, Antoine Louis presented his findings to the Assembly. His detailed report affirmed that with this machine, decapitation would be instantaneous, and that tests would be made before the instrument would be put to use on human beings. On the 15th of April, Charles-Henri performed his first experiments with the new machine using live sheep. On April 17, assisted by his son and his two brothers, Louis-Cyr-Charlemagne and Louis-Charles-Martin, Charles-Henri repeated his experiments in the courtyard of the hospital of Bicêtre on the cadavers of two men and one woman. Among the spectators were the doctors, Guillotin, Antoine Louis, Michel Cullerier, chief surgeon of Bicêtre, Philippe Pinel the famous alienist, and Georges Cabanis, as well as members of the Constituent Assembly and delegates from the Council of Hospitals of Paris.

In his eagerness to convince the Assembly that this method of execution was the most humane, Guillotin stressed the part that Antoine Louis had played in its design and construction, knowing that the deputies would be impressed by his name and reputation. The speech was so effective that at first the deputies (and all of Paris) believed that Louis had been its creator. It was promptly baptized "La Louison" or "La Louisette," and not until several weeks had elapsed did the world learn that the invention was Guillotin's.

The first execution of a human being took place in the place de Grève on the 25th of April at three o'clock in the afternoon. The victim was one Jacques Pelletier, condemned for theft. A report on it appeared in the *Journal de France*: "Yesterday La Petite Louison was used for the first time to cut off a head . . . a man named Pelletier was the sad victim." The journalist, Duplan by name, went on to describe his own feelings:

> Never in my life have I been able to go near a man who has been hanged, but I must confess that I am even more repelled by this method of execution. The preparations make one shiver, and intensify the mental suffering; as for the physical agony, I had heard that it would be as quick as the wink of an eye, but it seemed to me that the public was crying out for Monsieur Sanson to return to the methods of the *ancien régime* and bidding him to:

> *Rends-moi ma potence en bois*
> *Rends-moi ma potence.*

> (Give me back my gallows, of wood
> Give me back my gallows.)

This was an allusion to a popular song, the first of many that would be composed about the doctor. The most famous of these ditties, and the most widely known, points the finger of shame at the machine and its inventor.

Guillotin
Médecin
Politique
Imagine un beau matin
Que pendre est inhumain
Et peu patriotique

(Guillotin,
Doctor of
Politics
Imagines one lovely morning
That hanging is inhumane
And hardly patriotic)

Aussitôt
Il lui faut
Un supplice
Qui sans corde ni poteau
Supprime du bourreau
L'office

(Immediately
He needs
A means of execution
Which without rope or stake
Abolishes the hangman's
Office)

Et sa main
Fait soudain
La Machine
Qui simplement nous tuera

[87]

Et que l'on nommera
GUILLOTINE

(And his hand
Suddenly creates
The Machine
Which will kill us easily
And which is called
Guillotine)

The poor doctor was destined to go down in history not as a skilled physician, but as a household word for execution. His name entered the language as both noun and verb. His contention that he never had and never would witness an execution fell upon deaf ears; and whenever he walked the streets of Paris, passers-by struck the napes of their necks with the palms of their hands and winked at one another.

Paris caught guillotine-mania; women wore small silver or gold guillotines dangling from their ears, children played with toy guillotines. In one of the Girondin salons, a miniature mahogany guillotine was placed on the dinner table when dessert was served. A tiny doll, the head of which might be modeled in the likeness of Robespierre or Danton or another famous personage, was decapitated; a red liquid flowed from its neck and the ladies dipped their handkerchiefs into it—for each doll was actually a flacon containing a sweet liqueur. The mania spread to England, where it became fashionable to cut chickens' heads off with small guillotines. And Joseph-Ignace Guillotin came to be feared and hated as deeply as were the Sansons. In the words of Carlyle: "Unfortunate Doctor! For two-and-twenty years he, unguillotined, shall hear nothing but guillotine, see nothing but guillotine; then dying, shall through long centuries wander, as it were, a disconsolate ghost, on the wrong side of Styx and Lethe; his name like to outlive Caesar's."

Famous or infamous, his memory would also perpetuate and intensify that of Charles-Henri Sanson and his descendents.

During the three years between the storming of the Bastille on July 14, 1789, and the storming of the Tuileries Palace on August 10, 1792, the tempo of the Revolution accelerated with ever-increasing intensity. Politics and political opinion teetered on a seesaw of indecision and change. Uncertainty begat fear and fear begat suspicion.

The principal problem was that of drafting a constitution for France; there could be no constitution until the question of the vote could be resolved. Would it be a vote by estate, or a vote by head? If the estates met separately, as they had done in the past, the Third Estate, although its deputies represented over ninety-five percent of the population, might find itself outvoted by the other two. Deputies of the Third Estate obviously opposed separate meetings and invited nobles and clergy to meet with them. Some of the clergy agreed to the proposal, and a handful of nobles joined them. This gathering then declared itself to be the National Assembly; it later

[89]

changed its name to Constituent Assembly, designating its primary goal. Despite bitter differences, the deputies managed to agree on a constitutional or limited monarchy, on a representative assembly which would meet at regular intervals and control the financial affairs of France, on equality of taxation irrespective of class, and on recognition of the basic rights of citizens. Henceforth there was to be freedom from arbitrary arrest, freedom of speech and of the press, and trial by jury. But the nobility was divided. The interests of those living at Versailles differed widely from the needs and wants of those living on country estates. The clergy vacillated, taking sides first with one segment of the population and then with another, depending on which views fostered its own betterment; and the people grew ever more impatient and then doubtful of what might never come to pass. Vagrants, criminals, tramps, and brigands roamed the streets of Paris, unemployed, restless, apprehensive, and hungry. Fear stalked the provinces, where the peasants, suspecting that they might be robbed of their harvest, hated noble and commoner alike. Louis XVI, trying to walk the eggshell path between factions, made every possible mistake; and in his eagerness to bring peace to his troubled nation, he compounded his errors by bringing troops into Paris to maintain order.

The conservative group, which sat to the right of the President's box in the Assembly, consisted of nobility and clergy; in the center sat the various groups or clubs—the Jacobin Club, which in its early days advocated constitutional reform; the Cordeliers, whose members could not afford the high dues of the Jacobins; and a popular society whose members were all journalists. All of these moderates wanted a form of government modeled on the English parliamentary system. The preponderance of deputies sat on the left; such men as the Abbé Sièyes, Prince Talleyrand and Bertrand Barère; among them on the extreme left sat a small group whose hero was the lawyer and fierce proponent of revolution, Maximilien Robespierre. Such diversity of opinion in one room could only herald disaster.

The famous Declaration of the Rights of Man had contained every ingredient for the equality of man, but the completed constitution of 1791 stated that only citizens of a certain wealth could vote, and only wealthier citizens could serve as electors, so that once again the poor were denied the right to be heard. Both the Constituent and the subsequent Legislative Assembly were as dictatorial in their way as the monarchy had been; the only difference between the two regimes was that power had changed hands. The nobility lost to the bourgeoisie.

When the Constituent Assembly gave way to the Legislative, in October of 1791, the Jacobin Club, headed by Robespierre, moved over to the left. A new and aggressive party, led by a journalist named Jacques-Pierre Brissot, succeeded in attracting a great number of followers. This group, later to be known as Brissotins or Girondins, believed that the only answer to the menace of European intervention in the Revolution was to do away with the King. Brissot embarked on a vicious crusade against the monarchy, and because he became head of the Diplomatic Committee, he managed to usurp the power (granted by the constitution to the King) of negotiating with foreign nations.

In April of 1792 France declared war on Austria. Louis believed that war might curb the extremists within his realm, the military believed it could save the King, and the Girondins were convinced that it would unmask

[91]

Louis XVI as a counter-revolutionary. When reverses at the front resulted in depleted finances and new riots and disturbances among the populace, the Girondins saw their chance to blame Louis XVI for all the misfortunes and intensified their attack. (The King himself had contributed to their suspicion and hatred by his ill-timed and ill-fated flight to Varennes in June of 1791.) The monarchy was overthrown, the King imprisoned, the Legislative Assembly became impotent and was forced to decree a new election, and Paris was controlled by the mob. Extremists attacked the Tuileries and the famous September massacres ensued.

The National Convention which followed the Legislative Assembly proclaimed France a Republic, "one and indivisible"—a lofty idea, except that the deputies continued to be divided among themselves. The Girondins, who had been on the left in the Assembly, moved to the right; next to them sat the Center, or Plain, and the Jacobins, heretofore moderates, became the extreme left—Jean-Paul Marat, Georges-Jacques Danton, Camille Desmoulins, and Robespierre.

Small wonder that no one dared to trust his neighbor in a shifting climate such as this, that everyone affected a patriotism he might or might not feel, agreed with whatever theory his current companion might espouse. Statements considered harmless yesterday might today be interpreted as crimes against the state; and for such treason the penalty was hanging, and after 1792, the guillotine. With spies everywhere, the prisons were filled and it is not surprising that the job of Charles-Henri Sanson increased in importance, becoming more and more burdensome as the months passed.

Three executions signaled the beginning of the avalanche that would continue for five years. On February 8,

1790, Charles-Henri was ordered to hang the brothers Auguste-Jean and Anne Jean-Baptiste Agasse for forging banknotes, and on the 19th he was given his first political victim, the marquis de Favras.

Thomas de Favras, convicted of treason against the state, is alleged to have plotted the assassination of Bailly, former Finance Minister Jacques Necker, and the marquis de La Fayette, commandant of the National Guard, and the kidnapping of the King and the royal family. There were no witnesses for the prosecution, however, and the tribunal refused to hear any witnesses for the defense, a strange situation in view of the Assembly's proclamation of equality and justice for all. The victim was hanged at night by torchlight in the presence of a vast crowd, half of which shouted its approval at the hanging of an aristocrat, while the other half muttered angrily about a government that could boast of its leniency in punishing criminals not guilty of murder, and at the same time execute a man not even proven guilty.

Charles-Henri, aware of the crowd's sentiments, began to see the direction in which the wind was blowing and probably guessed what his own future might hold. In addition, he felt tired and his health had not been good. On September 13 he went to a notary and prepared his letter of resignation, which he sent to the authorities together with a request for the necessary documents naming his son to succeed him. Unfortunately his prognosis proved to be more accurate than his timing; the authorities themselves could no longer control the momentum of daily events. His resignation was either ignored or lost in the mass of paperwork flooding the government offices.

It is not unlikely that another reason prompted Charles-Henri's decision to resign. Despite his work with

Doctor Guillotin during the initial stages of the Revolution, he personally was still a symbol of royalty and the *ancien régime,* and as suspect as any aristocrat. Not only had he decapitated, beaten, and hung the enemies of the throne, but he had harbored a royalist press in his dwelling, actions which had not been forgotten by the Revolutionary powers. Charles-Henri Sanson might be a symbol of royalty, but he did not think that the same accusation could be leveled at his son. He must have been correct in his assumption, because although the Revolutionary leaders bided their time, waiting until anti-royalist feeling reached a peak, they did not attempt to harm young Henri. But after the storming of the Tuileries Palace on August 10, 1792, Charles-Henri and his brothers, Louis-Charles-Martin, the executioner of Tours, and Louis-Cyr-Charlemagne, then executioner of Versailles (both of whom were serving as his aides), were arrested and taken to the Conciergerie.

Fate favored the executioners with a sardonic smile. They might well have been guillotined; the only reason for their release was that their services were needed to guillotine another. Louis Collenot d'Angremont, administrative secretary of the National Guard, was scheduled for execution on August 21 for having fired on the people during the riots of August 10.

During the first few weeks of its existence, the guillotine had been set up at the place de Grève. Following the execution of Jacques Pelletier, it had brought death to three soldiers, convicted of having murdered a lemonade seller of the Palais Royal, and then to a trio of forgers. For the execution of d'Angremont, it was brought to the place de la Réunion (today the place du Carrousel) near the principal gate of the Tuileries Palace. It was this execution that caused Carlyle to write: "For, lo, the great

Guillotine, wondrous to behold, now stands there; the Doctor's *Idea* has become Oak and Iron; the huge cyclopean axe 'falls in its grooves like the ram of the Pile-engine,' swiftly snuffing-out the light of men!" It would fall three more times on the place de la Réunion before Charles-Henri took his instrument back to the place de Grève for an execution that would be one of the most tragic of his career.

Three men, the Abbé Sauvade, Vimal, and Guillot, were beheaded for forging *assignats,* promissory notes issued by the revolutionary government. John Moore reported the incident in his *Journal During a Residence in France,* published in London in 1794: "On the 27th of August, three men were beheaded for forging assignats. After the execution, it is customary to hold up the head, that it may be seen by the spectators. In performing this ceremony, the son of the executioner approached too near the edge of the scaffold, fell over and was killed on the spot before his father's eyes."

Gabriel, the younger of Charles-Henri's two boys, died instantly of a fractured skull. (Every scaffold thereafter would have a railing enclosing it on all sides.) Hardened as they were to death in its most violent forms, neither Charles-Henri nor his wife, Marie-Anne Jugier, ever recovered from this tragedy. Beginning on that August day, the executioner began to hate the Revolution and all that it stood for; his enthusiasm and pride turned to disgust, to loathing, and to dread. He is often quoted as having said that as the days passed, he felt more pleasure at seeing the heads of the revolutionaries fall than those of Louis XVI and Marie Antoinette.

Another August entry in John Moore's *Journal* reflects this point of view. "I should think it probable," wrote the English visitor to Paris, "that many of the citizens who

[95]

were violent patriots at the beginning of the Revolution are now tired of the disorderly state of affairs and think that supporting the King is the most likely way of obtaining that tranquility which they have much need of. . . ."

We know that the executioner longed for a more tranquil existence, an existence that was his before 1789; but his work had just begun. The next three years would be the busiest, not only in his career, but in the career of any executioner in history, with the exception of those in Nazi Germany.

The crescendo of horror that began with the storming of the Tuileries Palace on August 10, 1792, and ended with the death of Robespierre on July 28, 1794, is a lengthy and eventful one in the history books. Power teetered from one faction to another, laws were promulgated, revised, and repealed, and no one knew from one day to the next whether he'd be public idol or prisoner. But to the executioner of high justice, yesterday, today, and tomorrow had a terrible sameness. As he himself said: "The stage set is the same, only the actors change."

The Tribunal began its hearings between nine and ten in the morning, recessed at noon, and reconvened at two. Sometimes the sessions ended in the early afternoon, in which case Charles-Henri received his victims the same day. But if the debates and arguments continued until late at night, as frequently happened, executions were postponed until the following day. Charles-Henri arrived at the Palais de Justice (then known as the Maison de Justice) about ten o'clock in the morning and presented himself at the office of Antoine Fouquier-Tinville, the Public Prosecutor, which was on the first floor of one of the towers, overlooking the quai. Fouquier-Tinville gave him a list of those scheduled to appear before the Tribunal, and from that list, an estimate of those who would be condemned—an estimate which was rarely wrong. The reason for this briefing was so that Charles-Henri, who only had two tumbrels or carts at his disposal, could rent additional vehicles if necessary (at fifteen francs apiece, plus five francs tip for each driver) and so that he could hire assistants to supplement the four normally in his employ. During the Terror, he had as many as seven.

From time to time, his brothers, Louis-Charles-Martin and Louis-Cyr-Charlemagne, and his uncle Nicolas-Charles-Gabriel helped him on the scaffold, but they were not counted among the regulars.

For the most part, his known assistants belonged to families of executioners. The Desmorests, for instance, were sons of the executioner of Grenoble. Pierre, the older of the two, had been assistant to the executioner of Besançon. François Le Gros, a carpenter by trade, usually made whatever repairs were necessary to the scaffold, and it was he who would later gain fame by slapping the cheek of Charlotte Corday. Vermeille's family had been executioners in Amiens, Laon, Cambrai, Valenciennes, and his sons would become executioners at Lyon and Montpellier. Levasseur, called La Rivière, was a descendent of the La Rivière who had been replaced by the first Charles Sanson. Robineau would later be named executioner at Perpignan, from which post he returned to Paris to assist Charles-Henri's son.

All of these men were paid by Charles-Henri, and it is said that they also took watches, rings, lockets, and other valuables, not to mention articles of clothing, from the victims and sold them. An oft-told anecdote relates that one of the condemned men, upon seeing the clothing and jewelry discarded by several of his predecessors on the scaffold, turned to the executioner's aide and said: "My compliments, sir. You must have the most extensive wardrobe of any man in France."

After receiving his orders for the day, Charles-Henri either went home or (after October of 1792) attended to the public exhibition or viewing of prisoners convicted of theft, forgery, arson, crimes other than those against the state. Before this date, the questioner of Paris performed this duty, but after torture had been abolished, the task fell upon Charles-Henri. He had to see that the special scaffold was erected in the place de Grève, and then supervise the placing of the criminals, who were tied with straps and ropes, and had a sign hung about their necks giving their name, age, profession, and the nature of the crime they had committed. About three o'clock he returned to the Palais de Justice, dressed in his tricorn hat, his dark green redingote and striped trousers, ready for the formalities that preceded execution.

Accompanied by one or two of his aides, Charles-Henri went directly to the records office, where he was required to sign for his prisoners. From there, his footsteps continued to the *salle des morts*—the hall of the dead—a long, dark, narrow room where the condemned men, women, and children awaited him. Here the prisoners' hair was cut, and either sent to the bereaved

[98]

family or dropped into a wicker basket from which the wife of the concierge, the Femme Richard, is alleged to have taken the shorn locks and sold them to neighborhood wigmakers at a vast profit. Here, too, were the so-called Constitutional or juring priests, who heard the confessions of the condemned, although most men and women preferred going to their death without absolution from such apostates.

Then, their shirts or bodices slit at the neck, their wrists tied behind their backs, the victims proceeded to the prison courtyard, where Charles-Henri called out their names to the accompaniment of jeers and insults from a waiting crowd of *sans-culottes* and *tricoteuses* on hand to witness the humiliation of the hated aristocrats and traitors. The tumbrels were loaded with five or six victims each and escorted by mounted gendarmes, and the mournful procession set out for the scaffold.

The guillotine moved many times during the next years, from the place de Grève to the place de la Réunion; for one five-day period to the place Saint-Antoine in front of the ruins of the Bastille; for a month to the Barrière du Trône Renversé. For the execution of Bailly it operated on the Champ de la Fédération (now the Champ de Mars), but its longest tenure was on the erstwhile place Louis XV, renamed the place de la Révolution, today the place de la Concorde.

While the scaffold was erected on the place de la Révolution, where it remained the longest, the tumbrels always followed the same route. Upon leaving the Palais de Justice, they turned left and crossed the pont au Change, rolling along the quai de la Mégisserie, the rue de la Monnaie, the rue du Roule, the rue de la Convention (today the rue Saint-Honoré), then turned into the rue de la Révolution (today the rue Royale). In some instances they took the quai de l'Horloge and the pont Neuf to get to the rue de la Monnaie, but always approached the guillotine from the same angle.

The procession itself was heralded by criers distributing the newly printed list of the condemned. Hordes lined the streets, hurling obscenities at the victims and singing revolutionary songs. Every window was jammed with the curious, who pelted the red tumbrels with rotten fruit and vegetables. Some of the prisoners exhibited an admirable hauteur, choosing to ignore the mob or to throw scornful glances at the onlookers. Others sobbed, and many kept their eyes closed, their lips moving in silent prayer. Waiting at the scaffold were officers of the revolutionary tribunal, wearing the silver chain of office over their black habits. Near them stood the red cart, waiting to remove the bodies of the victims.

The number of curiosity-seekers and spectators gathered about the scaffold varied, depending on the importance of the victims, swelling when the names were well-known, diminishing when they were obscure. But usually the crowd was immense. A police report of the era describes the place de la Révolution as: "Filled with people running about like chickens without heads, so fearful of missing the spectacle that they were constantly on the move, trying to locate the best vantage point. Some climbed up on ladders, others on carriages and carts."

Charles-Henri and his aides lined the prisoners in rows with their backs to the scaffold. Their names were called and one at a time they mounted the steps to the guillotine, Charles-Henri on one side, his assistants on the other. The victim was forced to lie face down on the wooden plank or *bascule,* his neck imprisoned by the semi-circular halves of the collar known as the *lunette.* The

[100]

last sound he heard was the roar of the crowd as the guillotine's blade descended.

Burial of the victims also came under Charles-Henri's jurisdiction, but his aides attended to this task, which became increasingly difficult as the number of bodies swelled. In bringing the Church under state control, the Revolution had seized all of its land, including cemeteries. In 1792 only two remained: the Cimetière de L'Ouest or Vaugirard and L'Enclos de Clamart. In January of 1793, the day before the execution of Louis XVI, the Commune of Paris acquired a tract of land that had belonged to the ancient parish of the Madeleine, serving as a vegetable garden for the Benedictine nuns; and there the authorities ordered the digging of a trench ten feet deep, where bodies were thrown into a tomb of quicklime.

Charles-Henri organized, supervised, and directed; as Madame Roland would say of him: *"Il fait son métier et gagne son argent.* (He does his job and he earns his money.)" But after the initial weeks of the guillotine's existence, he took no part in the actual workings of the machine. His son Henri remarked that: "Since the invention of the guillotine, my father and I merely supervise. Everything is done by our assistants. During that dreadful epoch, we were so stunned that we fulfilled our function like robots, so numbed had we become to the procedure."

Henri Sanson neglected to mention the one notable exception—the execution of Louis XVI. No one but the executioner himself could perform this stern duty.

Louis XVI had been a prisoner in the Temple since the insurrection of August 10th, as were his Queen, his sister Madame Elizabeth, and his two children—Madame Royale, aged fifteen, and the Dauphin, aged eight.

He was no longer referred to as the King, but as Citizen Capet.

From August 10th to the proclamation of the Republic on September 22nd, France was neither a monarchy nor a republic. Danton, who had been elected Minister of Justice by the Legislative Assembly, dominated the government. But in reality three factions fought for power; the Legislative Assembly, the Provisional Executive Council, and the new Commune of Paris, of which Robespierre was a vociferous member. During this period, a mob massacred those of the Swiss Guards, the King's bodyguards, who had escaped with their lives from the Tuileries when it was captured for the Revolution. The statues of Henri IV, Louis XIII, and Louis XIV were pulled from their pedestals, and the populace of Paris and the provinces cried for vengeance against their oppressors. When it was learned on September 2nd that the Prussians and the Austrians had besieged Verdun, panic invaded the streets. It was then that Danton made his famous speech to the Assembly advocating *"de l'audace, encore de l'audace et toujours de l'audace"* in dealing with the invaders. The Assembly immediately declared everyone a traitor who refused to serve in the defense of Paris. But anger at the nation's foreign enemies proved no more intense than fear of the enemy within; conspirators and traitors—i.e., aristocrats and nonjuring priests—were thrown into prison by the hundred. Between September 2nd and 6th, over 1,100 people perished, and during the period which would be known as the September Massacres, Charles-Henri's guillotine operated from dawn until midnight.

Meanwhile the Legislative Assembly had given way to the Convention which postponed and procrastinated, refusing to make any decision as to the fate of the imprisoned Louis XVI. The Girondins were divided as to whether Louis should die, but the Jacobins or Mountain not only wanted him killed but were opposed to a trial, claiming that he already had been judged on August 10th and found guilty. Louis de Saint-Just thundered that to be a King was a crime in itself, and Robespierre echoed the sentiment, demanding that the Convention declare Louis a traitor to the French nation. In spite of these two orators, the Assembly voted to give Citizen Capet a trial, and he was brought before the Convention and called upon to answer thirty-three charges, most of them quite preposterous. Girondin and Jacobin argued and debated, the speeches continuing through November and December. Not until January 19th did the final and decisive vote take place. The verdict was death.

On December 14th of 1792, the president of the National Convention received a letter, supposedly written by Charles-Henri Sanson:

> The brothers Samson [*sic*], *exécuteurs des jugements criminels* of the department of the Seine, take the liberty of writing a letter to the National Convention; as they deem the matter of some importance, they beg that you will read this to the Convention.
>
> Deputies, you are about to decide the fate of our former King. His head is undoubtedly destined to fall beneath the blade which is mine to wield. Despite the prejudice, my job is an honorable one; I consider myself a bulwark of the law, a terror to criminals, and a useful citizen. Executioner of the Tribunals' judgments, I obey because it is my duty. But in the present situation, it is not unlikely that a tyrant destroyed will only

be succeeded by tyrants more unbearable and
more shameful. . . . I am availing myself of the
sacred right to which every individual is entitled,
to express my opinion, and to send you my
resignation, and that of everyone in my employ.
We are afraid of taking part in an assassination,
we fear the knowledge that our names, as well as
yours, will be forever damned by honest men;
moreover we dread the thought of being victims of
the certain and impending vengeance of a people
who will soon repent this useless crime. We are
convinced that you will easily find men equal to
our task. In the Convention itself, there will be
those only too eager to undertake it. Even now the
great Marat, Danton, Robespierre and many
others undoubtedly covet our job. We leave it to
them.
Your equals under the law
The executioners of criminal judgment of the
department of Paris.

The signature on this curious document is illegible. It
was found by Doctor Roger Goulard in the National
Archives, in a thick dossier devoted to petitions and
letters written to the Convention. In the opinion of
Doctor Goulard, it could not have been written by the
Sansons for several reasons: first of all, because only
Charles-Henri was entitled to be called *Exécuteur des
jugements criminels du département de la Seine* (his brothers
held the title in Tours and Versailles); and secondly,
because the name is spelled "Samson." But one might
well argue that the pride of this letter-writer no less than
his pompous mode of expression are quite in character
for Charles-Henri; the lines above the signature, "your
equals under the law," might well have been penned by

[104]

the executioner of Paris, who had spent a good deal of time fighting for just that right. The spelling of the name is not unheard of; it appears in the archives of the city of Soissons, and both Carlyle and Stefan Zweig refer to the executioner as "Samson." It is interesting, too, that the letter begins "the brothers Samson" using the plural pronoun in its first paragraph, then changes to the singular "I," only to end with a return to the initial "we." Charles-Henri was known to write adequate but not good French.

During the January days that preceded the execution of Louis XVI, Charles-Henri began to receive letters, some menacing, some pleading, some anonymous, some signed. He was warned that there would be an attempt made to save the King's life and that any interference on his part would cost him his life. Several writers offered to die in the King's place, and many implored Charles-Henri to refuse to execute the monarch.

On Sunday, January 20, 1793, the executioner received his orders; the execution would take place the following day on the place de la Révolution—the first time the guillotine would be placed here. Inasmuch as the orders contained none of the usual details, Charles-Henri wrote to the Prosecutor's assistant:

> Citizen:
>
> I have just received your orders. I shall see that they are carried out expeditiously. The carpenter has been alerted as to where to place the machine, which will be transported to the designated location.
>
> It is vital that I know how Louis will leave the Temple. Will there be a special carriage, or shall I use the ordinary cart? After the execution, what happens to the body?

Shall I go to the Temple, or send one of my aides? If I do not transport him from the Temple, where shall I await him?

None of these points were explained in my orders, and I should like to have answers to my queries as soon as possible, so that everything can be attended to with promptness and dispatch.

Charles-Henri received detailed answers to his questions: the execution would take place on the place de la Révolution between the pedestal of the statue of Louis XV (which had been knocked down a few months before) and the Champs Elysées. The executioner was not to go to the Temple but await his victim on the scaffold. The means of transport would be a closed carriage; instead of the executioner and his assistant, two gendarmes would accompany the King. This precautionary measure probably had been ordered for two reasons—the suspected royalist tendencies of Charles-Henri Sanson and the fury of the Parisian mob.

The scaffold was erected at five o'clock on the morning of January 21st; at eight o'clock, Charles-Henri, attired in his high hat, his dark green redingote, and a wide white cravat, left his house accompanied by his son Henri. Anticipating danger to themselves no less than to the person of Louis XVI, both father and son wore daggers and pistols concealed beneath their coats. Their assistants awaited them on the scaffold, and in the foggy, icy air of the January morning they tried out the *tranchoir* of the guillotine. Battalions of the National Guard surrounded the scaffold, while artillery guarded every bridge and every crossroads. Thousands thronged the place de la Révolution and choked the streets and byways leading to it. Every shop, every atelier, every boutique was shuttered. The only business transacted was that of street peddlers hawking their wares in the giant square itself.

The King's journey from prison to scaffold, his arrival, his last words, and his execution have been recounted variously—in the Sanson *Mémoires*, by eyewitnesses such as the Abbé Montgaillard, by John Moore, by le Citoyen Antoine Verité Windtsor, and by many others of the period. One of the most interesting of these accounts is that of the Abbé Edgeworth de Firmont, the King's confessor, who accompanied him from prison and was with him at his death.

Edgeworth was born in Ireland in 1745, the son of a convert to Catholicism. In 1749 the family moved to Toulouse, where Edgeworth received his early education before advancing to the Seminary in Paris. He became friend and confessor to Madame Elizabeth, the King's sister, by which means he became known to Louis XVI who grew to respect him deeply. That the King should have been permitted a confessor who was true to the faith instead of a member of the so-called constitutional clergy was perhaps due to the fact that the Abbé Edgeworth was an Irishman and not a Frenchman.

> The journey lasted almost two hours, [the Abbé wrote in his *Mémoires*]. Every street was lined with rows of armed citizens, some bearing shovels, some with guns. In addition, the carriage itself was escorted by an imposing number of troops, consisting undoubtedly of the most corrupt blackguards in Paris. To complete the precautionary measures, a multitude of drums preceded the horses, so that any shouting in favor of the King should be inaudible. But such would

have been impossible anyway. For there was no one, either in doorways or at windows or in the streets except armed citizens, that is to say citizens who, albeit because of weakness, conspired to a crime that perhaps they hated in their hearts.

The carriage advanced in hollow silence to the Place Louis XV, stopping in the center of a space that had been cleared near the scaffold. The area was encircled by cannons, and beyond it, as far as the eye could see, was a host of armed men. . . . One of the executioners came over to open the carriage door and the gendarmes started to get out; but the King stopped them. . . .

. . . As soon as the King had stepped out of the carriage, three executioners surrounded him, wanting to divest him of his clothing. But he repulsed them proudly and took off his outer clothing himself. He unfastened his collar, opened his shirt, and fixed it with his own hands. The executioners again approached him, wanting to bind his hands. "What do you want?" the King asked, pulling his hands away. "To tie you up," replied one of the executioners. "To tie me up?" the King repeated the words indignantly. "I shall never consent to that."

The steps leading up to the scaffold were very steep. The King was obliged to lean on my arm, and because of the effort it appeared to cause him, I feared for a moment that his courage had failed. Imagine my astonishment, when, having reached the last step, I saw him step away from me and walk firmly across the scaffold, his look alone silencing the roll of fifteen or twenty drums . . . and in a voice strong enough to be heard at the Pont-Tournant, speak the following forever-memorable words: "I die innocent of every crime of which I have been accused. I

[108]

forgive the perpetrators of my death and I pray
God that my blood will not fall upon France."

. . . The youngest of the executioners (he
looked to be under eighteen years old) seized the
severed head and made the rounds of the scaffold,
showing it to the populace. This monstrous ritual
was accompanied by loud shouting and obscene
gestures. A hollow silence ensued and shortly
afterward there were a few weak cries of "Long
live the Republic." But little by little the voices
multiplied and in less than ten minutes the cry,
repeated a thousand times became the unanimous
shout of a multitude. . . .

In a letter to his brother, Mr. Usher Edgeworth,
written in London in September 1796, the Abbé concludes the story:

All I can say is that as soon as the fatal blow was
given, I fell upon my knees and thus remained
until the vile wretch [Sanson] who acted the
principal part in this horrid tragedy, came with
shouts of joy, showing the bleeding head to the
mob, and sprinkling me with blood that streamed
from it. Then indeed, I thought it time to quit the
scaffold; but casting my eyes round about, I saw
myself invested by twenty or thirty thousand men
at arms; . . . all eyes were fixed on me, as you
may suppose. I was not permitted on this occasion
to wear any exterior marks of a priest. . . .

In some versions of·this tale, an attempt was made
near the porte Saint-Denis to rescue the King; in others
the cortège reached its destination without incident. In

an account by the Abbé Montgaillard, Louis's last words were interrupted by Santerre, Commandant of the *Garde Nationale,* who shouted: "I brought you here, not to harangue the populace, but to die."

The farewell phrase, *fils de Saint Louis, montez au ciel* (son of Saint Louis, ascend to Heaven), attributed to the Abbé Edgeworth and quoted by Carlyle and Thiers among others, may or may not have been uttered when the hapless King went to his death. When queried about it, Henri Sanson apparently shrugged his shoulders, replying: "It is possible that he spoke the words. I personally did not hear them."

According to Montgaillard, immediately after the King's head had fallen, "A furious populace invaded the scaffold, plunging its arms into the royal blood as if it were a talisman that would render those who touched it victorious over all the kings on earth." In the Sanson *Mémoires,* it was a citizen who climbed up onto the scaffold and, plunging his naked arm into the blood, sprinkled the group of executioner's aides. "Brothers," he exhorted them, "we were warned that the blood of Louis Capet would fall on our heads; well, let it fall; Capet washed his hands in ours often enough! Republicans, royal blood will bring us good luck."

Another eyewitness, this time a member of the guard, reports:

> Our battalion left the barracks at seven o'clock in the morning to surround the Place Louis XV; no sooner had the execution taken place, when about a hundred men and women formed a circle and danced for joy, singing the *chanson des Marseillais* at the top of their lungs, and shouting: "the tyrant's head has fallen." We also noticed that below the

scaffold, a number of people were washing their hands in the king's blood. This, of course, referred to what his wife [Marie Antoinette] had said about the revolution, that she wanted to wash her hands in the blood of the French people. Well, the opposite came true, it is the French who wet their hands in the blood of her husband.

The body of Louis XVI, which had arrived at the place of execution in a closed carriage, left it in the executioner's cart, the royal coffin a wicker basket. It was taken to the cemetery of La Madeleine and there thrown into a grave six feet wide and twelve deep, and covered with quicklime. Charles-Henri did not accompany it. Someone who had watched the cortège said that when the executioner's cart departed from the cemetery, the wicker basket fell to the ground. In seconds a crowd threw themselves upon it, rubbing handkerchiefs, shirts, or pieces of white paper around the inside of the basket—one person even rubbed a pair of gambling dice in the blood—everyone desiring a memento of the occasion.

There has been a good deal of argument as to who actually performed the execution, some claiming that Charles-Henri did it, others maintaining that it was his son. First of all, it seems highly unlikely that anyone but the executioner himself would have been permitted to decapitate such an important personage. Secondly, there are the words of Charles-Henri himself, who in 1806 informed Napoleon, "Sire, I executed Louis XVI." Thirdly, Henri Sanson is quoted as having said: "I was beside my father when he was forced to execute poor Louis XVI, a man much loved by our family. I was not the executioner at that time. My father still served in that capacity, but I acted as his assistant." And finally, if the details concerning the mutilation of the King's body can be considered evidence, Charles-Henri must have performed the decapitation. Only an inexperienced man (and Charles-Henri was inexperienced, having left all previous guillotinings to his aides) or a man whose innate disgust had made him timorous and consequently clumsy, could have performed the job so badly. The King's thick neck did not fit into the *lunette* properly, so that the guillotine blade that Louis himself had designed failed to complete its task. Charles-Henri's assistants had to throw their combined weight upon it after its descent, thereby increasing the wounds, the flow of blood—and the horror.

For several days following the execution, Charles-Henri Sanson was not seen about Paris. It was during this period that he is supposed to have ordered a mass for the soul of Louis XVI. In the preface of *Mémoires pour servir à l'histoire de la Révolution française* (published in Paris in 1829) by Henri Sanson, a work edited by Honoré de Balzac and Lhéritier de l'Ain, recounts the tale of a secret mass ordered by Charles-Henri Sanson; and in the fourth volume of *Scènes de la vie politique*, Balzac tells it again, under the title of "Un Épisode sous la Terreur." The story in brief is that on the night of January 22nd, a nun who had been forced to leave her convent like many others during the Revolution was walking along the faubourg Saint-Martin on her way to the attic dwelling she shared with another nun and a nonjuring priest. Suddenly she became aware that a man was following her. She had no sooner reached her lodgings when she heard a knock at the door. It was the unknown man, asking that the priest celebrate a mass for the soul of Louis XVI. After the priest had complied with this request, the stranger gave him a handkerchief stained with blood, then disappeared.

On the day following, the 9th of Thermidor, the priest found himself in front of a shop situated between the rue Saint-Roch and the rue des Frondeurs, when a large crowd emerging from the rue Saint-Honoré blocked his passage. "What's happening?" he asked the shopkeeper.

"Nothing," was the calm reply. "It's only the executioner and his cart en route to the place Louis XV for the execution of Robespierre and his accomplices."

The priest stared at the equipage, realizing with no small sense of shock that his mysterious visitor had been none other than Charles-Henri Sanson, executioner of Paris.

The truth of this story has never been proved or disproved, any more than the tale that every year on the 21st of January, Charles-Henri ordered expiatory masses said for Louis XVI in the church of Saint-Laurent. But it is known that after the loathsome January 21, 1793, every evening of his life he knelt down before the blade of the guillotine that had decapitated Louis XVI—a blade that was never used again—and prayed for the soul of the departed King.

Whether Charles-Henri was a royalist or merely a relic of the *ancien régime* is not important. A self-confessed snob, he had more than once called himself the chevalier de Longval. He served the King proudly and boasted of his two meetings with Louis XVI; he had permitted a royalist press to operate in his house. But he had also welcomed many of the new ideas and laws engendered by the Revolution and realized the necessity for reform, although like many others he grew to despise the violent methods used to enforce it. (At a later date he would confess that seeing the heads of the revolutionary leaders roll seemed to him more just than the execution of Louis XVI.) But more important than his political sentiments is the character of the man himself—an executioner, by profession, but paradoxically a kind, sensitive man, devoted to his family and to the life that surrounded him at home. His loyalty and affection for the King, the Queen, and all of the royal family is as undeniable as his growing distaste for his job. A proud man, he had learned to accept his public position, but he never learned to tolerate attacks upon his personal dignity and self-respect. The execution of Louis XVI resulted in just such an attack.

On January 29, 1793, a small article appeared in the *Thermomètre du jour,* in which the writer stated that:

> The buttons, the tattered pieces of his coat, the shirt of Louis Capet and his hair were gathered up and sold for enormous prices to collectors. The executioner, Sanson, accused of having participated in this new kind of commerce, has written to journalists denying the charge; here are his words: "I have just learned about the ugly rumor that accuses me of selling or allowing to be sold, the hair of Louis Capet. If it was sold, the infamous deed could only have been perpetrated by rogùes; the truth is that neither I nor any one of my associates took so much as one strand of it."

Another article, dated February 13th and entitled "Anécdote très exacte sur l'exécution de Louis Capet,". remarked upon the King's initial courage upon the scaffold, attributing it to the large dinner Louis had eaten the night before the execution and an equally large breakfast consumed the morning of the event. But, the article continued, at the first roll of the drums, the King's courage vanished and three times he called out, "I am lost." The writer of this tidbit claimed that he had received this information from none other than Sanson himself.

On February 18th, Dulaure, editor of the *Thermomètre du jour*, denied authorship of this article and requested that Charles-Henri send him an account of what actually happened. Charles-Henri's response was prompt and his defense of Louis XVI was printed on February 21st, one month after the execution.

> Here, in accordance with my promise, is the exact truth of what happened at the execution of Louis Capet.
>
> When he got out of the carriage, he was told to take off his coat; he demurred, saying that the execution could perfectly well be executed dressed the way he was. When informed that this was impossible, he himself helped us to divest him of his coat. The same situation was repeated when it became a question of binding his hands, and again when it was explained to him, he cooperated. He then asked if the drums would continue to roll, and we answered that we did not know, which was the truth. He climbed onto the scaffold and stepped forward as if to speak; but we told him that was forbidden. He then permitted himself to be led to the place where we fastened him down, and said in a clear voice: "My people, I die innocent." Afterward he turned back to us and said: "Messieurs, I am innocent of everything of which they accuse me. I can only hope that my blood will cement the happiness of the French people."
>
> These, citizen, were his true and last words.

[115]

> . . . To pay homage to the truth, he sustained
> all of this with a sang-froid and a strength that
> astonished us. I am convinced that he derived this
> strength from the tenets of his religion, because no
> one could have been a greater believer than he.
>
> [Signed:] SANSON,
> executioner of Criminal Justice

On January 23rd the news of Louis XVI's execution reached England with the impact of a thunderbolt. Both Court and Parliament went into mourning, theaters were closed, and Prime Minister William Pitt denounced the event as an "odious and atrocious" crime. When King George III appeared in public, his people greeted him with loud cries of "War on France."

The government in Paris had already made good its threat to spread the principles of revolution to every country in Europe by pushing the Austrians and Prussians back to the Rhine and by annexing Belgium. England realized that Holland would be next. With both Belgium and Holland in French hands, France would control all of the important commercial ports in the Low Countries, a serious danger to England's merchant fleet. Lord Grenville, the Foreign Secretary, sent a stern note to Paris condemning the government's aggressive policies and warning the French that the violation of the rights of other governments must cease.

Anger and resentment flared in the National Convention at the high-handed attitude of the English, and on February 1st, France declared war on England and Holland. Within a few months, England, Spain, Austria, Portugal, Naples, Tuscany, Sardinia, the Papal States (and ultimately, Russia and Prussia), had formed a coalition, plunging Europe into a war that would last for more than twenty years.

[116]

Inside France there was strife everywhere, not only in the Convention itself, but within the ranks of nobility, clergy, bourgeoisie, and peasantry, both in Paris and in the provinces. Everyone was disillusioned with the slow progress of the Revolution and the unfulfilled promises of the revolutionary leaders. Social unrest and discontent were increased by the sudden need to recruit an army, and rebellion broke out in more than one locality. (The Vendée, in the west of France, organized a revolt that blazed into civil war.)

On March 10th a revolutionary tribunal was established to punish all conspirators, and a decree was issued stating that crimes against the people would be punished by death. An "enemy of the people" meant anyone who dared to whisper against the National Convention and the revolutionary government—in fact anyone who expressed displeasure or discontent of any kind. The slightest remark was reported to the authorities, and the only proof necessary to condemn a man was a document containing accusatory statements. If such a document were presented, no witnesses would be heard. A single indictment often cited fifty to sixty individuals, none of whom had anything more in common than the fact that they'd been accused. People were condemned, judged, and guillotined—rapidly and en masse. The grand inquisitor of this tribunal was Fouquier-Tinville, the Public Prosecutor.

On April 6th, an executive committee of nine was created—the famous or infamous Committee of Public Safety—led initially by Danton (and much later by Robespierre) to deal with matters of internal and external safety and defense. This group, which would exist from April 1793 to October 1795, caused so much blood to be spilled that the ground on the place de la

Révolution could not absorb it, and in many parts of the square the earth became as soft as a quagmire.

For Charles-Henri Sanson, the brief period immediately after the execution of the King proved relatively quiet. In his own words: "The guillotine was at rest, as if she needed to gather her forces for the terrible work ahead." From the 25th of January until the 6th of April the guillotine claimed only one man, a deserter named Bukals, but in April Charles-Henri's activity began to quicken, and would accelerate rapidly from that time onward.

While the Revolutionary Tribunal became progressively more and more obsessed with the vocabulary of death, Charles-Henri, like the rest of the Parisian populace, was faced with the difficult problem of living. Ever since the abolition of feudal rights denied him the *droit de havage,* his income had dwindled considerably. In June of 1792 and again in August he had written to Roederer, enumerating his expenses and pleading for help. His medical practice brought some money into his coffers and the sale of cadavers to surgeons added a bit more, but with a large family to house, feed, and clothe, he found himself in desperate financial straits. In March 1792, the Minister of Justice was shocked by the pitiful situation of the Sansons and other executioners, all of whom had suffered privation with the abolition of *havage.* He asked the National Assembly to reduce the number of executioners to one per department and to grant pensions to those who would be forced to retire, but no action was taken.

Not until June 13, 1793, did the National Convention see fit to remedy the executioners' plight. A decree of that date ordered that henceforth there would be one executioner for each department of the Republic and that all

The Sanson coat of arms. The cracked bell explains the punning motto "Sans Son"—Without Sound

The law required that the executioner keep his distance from the rest of the populace, and so the house of Louis-Cyr-Charlemagne Sanson, Executioner of Provins, was situated outside the town walls on a narrow lane called the Allée du Bourreau (BARBARA LEVY)

Desrues broken on the wheel on the place de Grève. After a few blows, the executioner usually strangled his victim (NEW YORK PUBLIC LIBRARY PICTURE COLLECTION)

The pillory at Les Halles, in which the culprit—in this case, Gruet, a swindler—was rotated so as to be visible from all sides (NEW YORK PUBLIC LIBRARY PICTURE COLLECTION)

L'estrapade, a method of interrogation (or *question extraordinaire*) in which the prisoner was suddenly dropped from a great height, dislocating his joints (NEW YORK PUBLIC LIBRARY PICTURE COLLECTION)

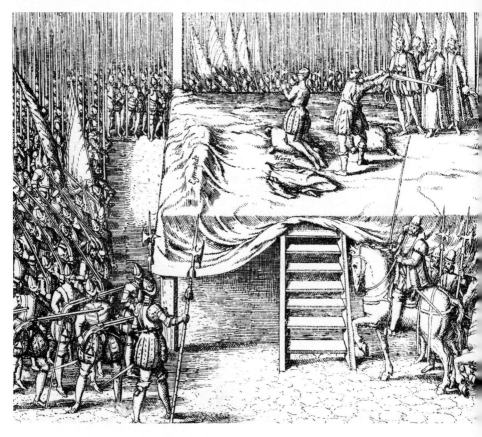

Members of the nobility had the "privilege" of being decapitated by a sword. Here the condemned is the comte de Horn who, in reality, was broken on the wheel for murder. The anonymous artist was apparently more influenced by the comte's rank than by the actual reports of the execution (NEW YORK PUBLIC LIBRARY PICTURE COLLECTION)

The "Sufferings of Damiens" who had tried to assassinate Louis XV. According to this contemporary woodcut, Damiens was first interrogated on a spiked chair (top right) and with a brazier under his feet (lower left). At the execution, his right hand was burned in sulphur (lower right) and boiling liquids poured in his wounds (top left). He was then drawn and quartered and his remains burned (center panels) (BIBLIOTHEQUE NATIONALE)

The Palais de Justice and the Conciergerie Prison on the Ile de la Cité (PHOTOGRAPHIE BULLOZ)

The Prison of Sainte Pelagie, from a sketch by Hubert Robert in the Musée Carnavalet. Prisoners who could afford it were lodged in quite comfortable "cells" with good food and even valet service (PHOTOGRAPHIE BULLOZ)

Duplessis' portrait of Louis XVI,
now in the Musée de Versailles
(PHOTOGRAPHIE BULLOZ)

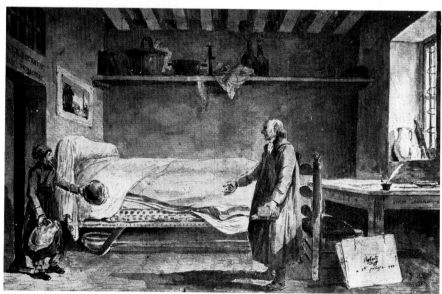

Marie-Antoinette; a detail of Mme. Vigée Lebrun's portrait in the Musée de Versailles (PHOTOGRAPHIE BULLOZ)

Josephe Ignace Guillotin, who consulted Charles-Henri Sanson on an "egalitarian" means of capital punishment (BIBLIOTHEQUE NATIONALE)

executioners' salaries would be paid by the state. In towns with a population of less than fifty thousand, the executioner would receive 2,400 livres; in towns with a population of fifty to one hundred thousand, four thousand livres; populations of 100,000 to 300,000, six thousand livres. The executioner of Paris would be paid ten thousand livres (a reduction of six thousand from the salary granted him by the Regent) plus one thousand livres for each of his assistants. In addition, whenever he had to perform an execution outside of Paris, he might claim expenses of twenty *sous* per league, which sum was to cover the transport of his guillotine.

The result of this decree, which became law in July, was chaos, confusion, and bitterness. In its eagerness to purge France of all aristocrats, the Committee of Public Safety hired executioners where it would and sent them out without consideration for either the individual's problems or the situation in a given locale. The job at Tarbes in the Haute Pyrenées was assigned to a man named Spirkel, whose entire family had been executioners in Montenach in Lorraine. He had seven children, spoke only the German patois of northeastern France, and Tarbes for him would have been not only exile but ruin. He refused the position. Many like him were uprooted from their native provinces and sent hundreds of miles only to find that the job was filled by a local citizen who refused to surrender it. Some men who had held the title of executioner for years were simple peasants who had never actually performed an execution and were too terrified to accept the position of executioner for an entire department.

A petition written by Charles-Henri and signed by all of the provincial executioners was sent to the Convention. The decree of June 13th, they declared, made it impossible for them to continue in the performance of their duties. They asserted that they had sacrificed everything for the good of the Revolution and that they hoped the decree would be revoked, inasmuch as the salary it granted them would not permit them to meet the cost of living. Charles-Henri must have succeeded in reaching the ear of an influential citizen, for in November a new decree granted a supplementary salary to the executioners of criminal justice. (This decree was dated 3 Frimaire, an II, or November 23, 1793.)

In addition to the sum granted in June, each executioner would now receive 1,600 livres for his two assistants, or eight hundred livres apiece. The executioner of Paris would be paid for four aides at one thousand livres each and would receive a supplementary sum of three thousand livres a year, so long as the government remained revolutionary. Article Two of this document stated that the cost of transporting the guillotine would be paid by the public treasury, and Article Three ordered that the sum of thirty-six livres be paid to any executioner who had to travel outside his own town or city in pursuit of his duty; and it specified one day for the journey to his destination, one day on which he performed his execution, and one day for the return—at twelve livres per day. Finally, each executioner deprived of a livelihood because of the reduction in their number (one for each department) was to receive a pension of one thousand livres a year.

Despite these improvements, Charles-Henri's financial situation continued to be difficult. In April 1794, during the Terror, he again petitioned the Minister of Justice, explaining that he now had the expense of seven assistants, none too many considering the amount of work involved, and that unless he guaranteed board and lodging, no one would work for him. The additional personnel involved the renting of another house at three thousand livres a year, and in view of these burdensome costs, he did not have enough money left to support himself and his family. If the situation continued, he would be obliged to resign. Fouquier-Tinville, aware of the truth of the executioner's statements, took them to the Committee of Public Safety and secured him a bonus of twenty thousand livres. In June 1795, Charles-Henri would write again, this time pleading for money to pay for the two carts that he had to have at his disposition every day, because drivers for these carts now asked the exorbitant price of one hundred livres a day.

These requests for money were far from unreasonable, as Charles-Henri's profession turned into a business and execution became wholesale murder. This turn of events began with the dissolution of the first Committee of Public Safety and the election of a new one on July 10, 1793. Several members of the old committee were reelected, but Danton, the most important one, was not. His relatively moderate and conciliatory attitude was replaced by the aggressive, belligerent, blood-soaked fanaticism of the Jacobins and their idol, Maximilien Robespierre, who believed that repressive measures were the only means of rescuing France from the dissension and treason that prevailed within her borders. Three days after the new committee took office, an event occurred which convinced its members of the rightness of their theories and intensified their policy of repression— the murder of Jean-Paul Marat.

Marat, a physician who had abandoned science for politics in 1789, founded a newspaper called *L'Ami du peuple* in which he attacked the *ancien régime,* the King, and all those in power. His articles grew more and more inflammatory as the Revolution progressed, his Jacobin views emerging in the Convention, where his oratory was a thundering denunciation of the Girondins and their policies of moderation. Marie-Anne Charlotte Corday d'Armont, a young girl from the province of Normandie, believed fervently in the principles and ideals of the Revolution and had espoused the cause of the Girondins with all the zeal and the romanticism of youth. In her eyes, Marat was to blame for all the misfortunes of France, and she convinced herself that if he were to die, peace and harmony would be restored to her country. Leaving her home in Caen, she arrived in Paris on July 11th and went directly to a shop in the Palais Royal, where she purchased an ebony-handled knife. As the world knows, she found her victim in his bathtub and plunged the knife into his defenseless body. Imprisoned in the Conciergerie and condemned to death by the Revolutionary Tribunal, she was delivered to Charles-Henri Sanson on the 17th of July.

The execution of Charlotte Corday was not the first or last time when Charles-Henri's gentleness and kindness were so striking as to win him the strange epithet of *le bourreau humanitaire.* Upon arriving at the Conciergerie he was met by the wife of Richard, (the famous "concierge" of the prison), whose extreme pallor caused him to inquire if she were ill. "Just wait," she replied. "Your heartache will be even greater than mine." The meaning of her words became clear to the executioner the moment he entered the girl's prison cell, for she was young enough to be his daughter. After he had cut her hair, he informed her that he must bind her hands, and she merely nodded, asking very calmly if she might be permitted to wear gloves so that the straps would not cut her wrists. Touched by her beauty and by her incredible display of courage, Charles-Henri put the straps away and left her arms free. Once in the tumbrel she said she preferred to stand up, and the executioner once again chose to disregard his orders. "That's a good idea," he told her. "For if you stand up, the jolting of the cart will be less tiring."

Along the route to the guillotine, he could not help noticing her nervousness and gave her a compassionate smile. "It's long, isn't it?" he said.

Her response, spoken with a sad smile, melted his heart. "Yes, but at least we're sure of reaching our destination." The account of that journey is best told in his own words.

> In a window of the rue Saint-Honoré, I recognized citizens Robespierre, Camille Desmoulins, and Danton, deputies to the Convention. Citizen Robespierre appeared to be very animated, and spoke at length to his colleagues, but the latter, especially citizen Danton, didn't seem to be listening very attentively; their eyes were fixed upon the condemned. I myself kept turning around to look at her, and the more I gazed at her, the more I wanted to gaze. This was not because of her beauty, although she was very beautiful, but because I couldn't believe that right up to the end she could remain as sweet and as courageous as she had been. . . .
>
> She didn't speak, she ignored those who surrounded the tumbrel shouting obscenities and filth at her, but she did look at the horde of citizens lined up in front of every house. There was such a crowd in the street that our progress was very slow. . . .

> When we reached the place de la Révolution, I
> got out and stood in front of her so that she should
> not see the guillotine, but she leaned forward and
> peered around me, saying: "I have the right to be
> curious, I've never seen one before."
> . . . I thought it would be barbarous to
> prolong, even for a second, the agony of such a
> courageous woman.

The episode that followed her execution has been told many times, and appears in most of the contemporary accounts. François Le Gros, a huge brute of a man and a carpenter by trade, often served as one of Charles-Henri's aides. Because he'd been repairing the scaffold that afternoon, he was present at Charlotte Corday's execution. After the guillotine had severed her head, he bent down and seized it. Holding it high, he toured the scaffold, brandishing it before the populace, and slapping the cheeks vigorously several times. This revolting procedure enraged even the most bloodthirsty of the spectators, all of whom roared their indignation and anger. Charles-Henri, sickened by his assistant's actions, gave him a swift punch and discharged him on the spot. (Le Gros was not only admonished by the chief of police, but later arrested by the Revolutionary Tribunal and severely punished.)

But the most interesting part of the story is that many of the spectators swore that they had seen a blush color the cheeks after Le Gros had slapped them. Michelet explains this phenomenon as an optical illusion, caused by the red rays of the setting sun shining through the trees on the Champs Elysées; Villiers claims that what the crowd saw was the bloodstained hands of the executioner; but hindsight is always simple, and neither of these men was alive at the time.

The Marquise de Créquy (or more properly Renée-Charlotte-Victoire de Froullay de Tessé, marquise de Créquy, de Heymont, de Canaples), one of the most intelligent and wittiest women of her time (her husband was one of Louis XIV's godsons and her son married Madame de Sévigné's granddaughter), lived through the Revolution, and her *Mémoires* report the incident, and an opinion regarding the blush that suffused a dead woman's cheek.

. . . They said that her [Corday's] head which one of the executioner's aides had had the infamous disrespect to slap when showing it to the populace, looked as if it had come back to life, and as if she had thrown him a look of anger and indignation. Dr. Séguret, erstwhile professor of anatomy, a very able and conscientious personage . . . assured us that such a thing was possible. He told us that he had been asked to conduct experiments on the effects of the guillotine; that he had had sent to him the remains of several criminals immediately after their death and that he had reported the following results.

We exposed two heads to the sun's rays and we opened the eyelids. The eyelids promptly closed, of their own accord, and with an aliveness that was both abrupt and startling. The entire face then assumed an expression of intense suffering. One of these heads had an open mouth from which the tongue protruded. When a student in surgery decided to prick the tongue with the point of his lancet, it withdrew into the mouth and the facial features grimaced as if in pain. Another of the guillotine's victims, an assassin called Terier, was subjected to similar tests, and more than a quarter of an hour after decapitation, his eyes turned in the direction of a man who was speaking.

Le Père Guillou told me that he had spoken personally with the older Sanson, . . . who told him that the head of a member of the National Convention and Juring priest called Gardien had been placed in the same sack with the head of another Girondin called Lacaze, and had bitten it with such fierceness and strength that it proved impossible to separate them. . . .

". . . The guillotine is one of the most horrible and most inhumane kinds of death that has ever been invented," said Dr. Séguret (into my ear so that the weak should not be frightened). The agony that follows decapitation is excruciating, and I firmly believe that it continues until all heat has left the body. This philanthropic invention is easy to operate, swift, advantageous to the French republic and above all convenient for the executioner, but no one can say that it is either advantageous or convenient to the condemned, because it is certain that strangulation cannot be as painful.

The marquise de Créquy is not the only person to write of bodies reacting after death; others claim to have seen headless corpses arise ten minutes after execution, walk about the scaffold and then collapse, their bodies convulsed in the final death agonies. Whether or not Charles-Henri either witnessed or believed these tales, they were known to him, and must have haunted his waking moments as well as his dreams.

But the real nightmare was yet to come.

The so-called Reign of Terror, which
claimed more than twenty thousand victims, began in
October of 1793 and was not to end until the death of
Robespierre in July of 1794. It was, in fact, a period of
dictatorship, governed by a tyrannical oligarchy, the
Committee of Public Safety, which controlled ministers,
Convention, and populace. National unity was to be
achieved by stamping out all those who opposed the
Revolution, and the definition of such traitors was spelled
out in the dread Law of the Suspects, passed on
September 17, 1793.

Who were the suspects? Those who in any way
threatened the Republic—aristocrats, priests, advocates
of moderation (Girondins), all those who, while they may
have committed no specific crime *against* the state, had
done nothing *for* it. This law, like the *ancien régime's lettres
de cachet,* could and would be used as a means of settling
personal grudges and private jealousies. To enforce it,
small revolutionary committees were organized, one for
each commune or district in the provinces, one for each
of forty-eight sectors in Paris. These committees drew up
lists of "suspects" within their districts, arrested them,
seized their papers, and sent their names to the central
committee, which in turn imprisoned them and ordered
their deaths. Spies lurked on every street corner and in
every shop, for the enemies of this Jacobin dictatorship
included royalists, constitutional monarchists, clergy,

[127]

republicans of moderate views, and in the end, factions within the Jacobin party itself.

A collection of reports, entitled *Rapports des agents secrets du Ministre de l'Intérieur*, gives some indication of the kind of information that reached the authorities almost daily during the Reign of Terror. The report of Grivel, dated September 11th, 1793 says: "There was bread left over in almost all of the bakeries today; in spite of all the arrests that have been made, the public seems quiet; there were quite a goodly number of gatherings in the Tuileries today, but they were small groups, and talk was quiet. A few suspicious looking characters tried to stir up trouble by talking about how much bread would be distributed today. . . ."

The report of Latour-Lamontagne suggests that the ministry set a watch on all gambling houses, which had multiplied in recent days, and which, he says, were undoubtedly one of the causes of misery. He also says that the theaters were "infected" with members of the aristocracy. An agent called Soulet writes that a group of women got into a fight in front of a bakery. Almost every report mentions bread, some claiming there was indeed a shortage, and others denying it. Grivel writes again on September 13th, saying: "In many sectors of Paris, people have started to congregate in front of bakeries again. In some places, many have had to go away without bread. One group, which gathered in front of a bakeshop on the faubourg Saint-Honoré near the Hôtel de Beauvau, was composed largely of shrill-voiced, tough women, whom we suspect of being agitators. We threw water on them, and this caused them to disperse." Complaints about shortages of food could also be interpreted as a betrayal of the Republic, although it was only the severity of winter climate and the hunger which accompanied it that produced these gatherings of desperate people.

Charles-Henri's tumbrels clattered down the cobbled streets from dawn to midnight as October's chill winds bared the trees on the Champs Elysées. General Custine, who had fought in the American Revolution, was accused of treason and guillotined. Philippe d'Orléans, who had renamed himself Philippe Égalité when the monarchy fell, was arrested, and in the official words: *"La Convention Nationale a décrétée aussi que la scélérate Antoinette serait jugée cette semaine. Vive la Montagne!* (The National Convention has also decreed that the villainous Antoinette will be judged this week. Long live the Mountain!" [i.e., the Jacobins in the Convention]

The Queen, imprisoned in the Conciergerie since she had been transferred there from the Temple on August 2nd, would undergo the humiliation of appearing before the Tribunal and of hearing herself charged with a long and outlandish list of crimes against the state. In the words of the prosecutor, Fouquier-Tinville: "Since her residence in France, Marie Antoinette, widow of Louis Capet, has been the curse and the leech of the French people." The final indignity was the charge that she had had sexual intercourse with her son, the Dauphin, who was only eight years old at the time. The verdict of the Convention was unanimous—death, each member of the jury aware that a vote for her life might cost him his own.

The effect of the verdict on the Sanson household is recorded in Henri Sanson's family annals: "Condemned! she is condemned just as he was!" cried Marie-Anne, the wife of Charles-Henri. "So much innocent blood on our hands, and on the hands of our children."

"The blood is not on our hands, but on those responsible for ordering it shed; and they shall answer to man and to God," was the executioner's reply.

"A pretty fine distinction, Charles. If you knew what I suffered, the day of the King's death, you wouldn't be a party to this second murder."

But Charles-Henri received his orders from the Tribunal, and those orders had to be obeyed, regardless of his personal sentiments, and those of his wife and family. On the morning of October 16th, after having inspected the guillotine on the place de la Révolution, Charles-Henri went to the Conciergerie, accompanied by his son. At seven o'clock in the morning, he was taken to the Queen. According to Henri, she greeted Charles-Henri saying, "You are early, Monsieur. Couldn't you wait a little longer?"

The executioner's reply was brief. "No, Madame. I must obey my orders."

The Queen's hair, which had turned white during her long imprisonment, had already been cut. Henri Sanson tied her hands behind her back and the procession began. Charles-Henri followed his royal victim, holding the ends of the rope that bound her wrists. According to an eyewitness, the executioner's feelings were visible; he let the rope dangle loosely as they crossed the courtyard of the Conciergerie, he helped his prisoner up the narrow ladder and into the tumbrel with a deference and a solicitude more suitable to the Palais de Versailles than the Palais de Justice. He had asked Fouquier-Tinville whether she should be taken to the scaffold in a closed carriage such as the one used for Louis XVI; the Public Prosecutor had instructed him to use an ordinary tumbrel, saying it would be quite good enough for "the Austrian woman."

Marie Antoinette seated herself facing the horse, but Charles-Henri, torn with pity, turned her around so that she should not see what lay ahead of her. The Abbé Girard, a constitutional priest, dressed in nonclerical garb, sat down beside her on the wooden plank and tried to talk to her as they jolted out of the courtyard of the Palais de Justice. She made no reply. Several times during the long journey Charles-Henri signaled the priest to leave her alone with her thoughts, but to no avail. "But Madame," the priest said at last, "what will people say when they learn that you have refused the solace of your religion at your hour of death?"

"If anyone should ask you," said Marie Antoinette, "you may say that God's infinite mercy is assured."

The guillotine had been erected between the statue of Liberty and the entrance to the Tuileries gardens, so that the Queen's last view should be that of the royal palace.

"Courage, Madame," Charles-Henri said to her as she got out of the tumbrel.

"Thank you, Monsieur," she replied calmly.

Prud'homme, reporting the execution of the Widow Capet in his *Révolutions de Paris*, says that: "In mounting the scaffold, Antoinette accidentally trod on the foot of citizen Sanson, causing the executioner sufficient pain for him to cry 'Aie.' She turned to him, saying, 'Monsieur, I beg your pardon. I did not do it on purpose.'" This incident has been mentioned in more than one contemporary account, but the journalist, unlike others, does not attribute it to the instinctive good manners and natural courtesy of royalty. He adds: "It is probable that she [Marie Antoinette] contrived this little scene so as to assure herself that her name would be remembered. Certain people never lose their *amour-propre;* one may say that that holds true for all court personages."

According to Henri Sanson, the Queen looked out at the Tuileries Palace and sighed once or twice. "We didn't disturb her, we gave her all the time she wanted," he states. In his opinion, Marie Antoinette maintained her dignity and her nobility right up to the last second.

The marquise de Créquy's memoirs are a little more emotional, which might be expected from a woman and an aristocrat:

> Marie Antoinette of Lorraine and of Austria, Queen Mother and dowager of France and Navarre, was born on November 2, 1755, and died on the scaffold on October 16, 1793. Her widow's weeds were in shreds, so the wife of the jailer dispensed the charity of a skirt and a blouse of white cotton. She was taken to the place of execution in a cart, her hands tied behind her back with a piece of bloodstained rope. Beside her was a constitutional priest whose help she had refused and to whom she now turned a deaf ear. She seemed exhausted by the weight of her sorrow; her eyes were fixed on some distant horizon, her cheeks flushed as if with fever. When the executioner (who was not the older Sanson) ripped the scarf that covered her shoulders and breast, she pulled away from him with a show of regal displeasure that seemed to intimidate him; but immediately thereafter the august victim lowered her eyes without speaking. One could see her lips move in silent prayer. . . .
>
> . . . I don't know how I have found the strength to write these details. They were told me by the Abbé du Puget, who was stationed along the route taken by the Queen, at the intersection of the rue Royale and the place Louis XV, so that

he could give her absolution *in articolo mortis*. . . .
A way had been found of letting her Majesty
know about this, but they forgot to tell her that
the almoner of the late King would be standing
on the left. . . . She was staring directly ahead at
the Hôtel de Coislin, and recognizing no one, she
suddenly turned her head. Her expression
changed to one of beatific joy when she saw the
venerable figure of M. du Puget, who had climbed
onto a pile of stones, holding up a crucifix so that
she could see it and receive his blessing.

Madame de Créquy's reference to an executioner "who was not the older Sanson" probably meant that Charles-Henri's repugnance for the guillotine and his distress over the royal status of his victim were such that he ordered his son to perform the actual execution. Accounts by the Abbé Edgeworth, the Abbé Carrichon, and Montgaillard confirm the fact that it was a young man who guillotined the Queen. (Charles-Henri at that time was fifty-four years old.)

Lapierre, a citizen who witnessed the execution, leaves a different version:

Marie Antoinette the bitch came to as pretty an
end as any pig at Godille's, our neighborhood
pork butcher. She went to the scaffold manifesting
incredible strength the entire length of the rue
Saint-Honoré; she crossed Paris, looking at the
crowd with scorn and disdain, and everywhere she
went, the true *sans-culottes* screamed "Vive la
République" and "Down with Tyranny!" The
hussy had the effrontery to go to the scaffold
without flinching, but when she saw the
instrument of her fate, she fell to her knees."

[133]

The crowd was brutal in its enthusiasm, the wits of the day cruel in their indictment. One of the many popular songs composed in honor of the event filled the air of the capital city in the days preceding the Queen's death.

Contre Antoinette la veuve
La France ne fit qu'un cri
Elle subit la même épreuve
Que le Sire son mari
A mater cette ex-Reine
Le fer n'a point réussi
La Majesté souveraine
S'y montrait en raccourci

Against the widow Antoinette
France raised one common cry
She underwent the same ordeal
As His Majesty her husband
The iron could not manage
To break this former Queen
Her sovereign Majesty
Made very little of it.

Another of these songs, sung to the accompaniment of a popular tune called "Ports à la Mode," followed Charles-Henri as his tumbrel made its daily rounds.

Demain Sanson, d'un air benêt
Me dira: Faut que je tonde
Tu pourras, l'ami s'il te plaît
Terroriser dans l'autre monde

J'acheterais des têtes
Si j'avais les moyens
J'en porterais en fêtes
Une dans chaque main.

[134]

A sketch of the model of the original guillotine, now in the Musée Carnavalet (PHOTOGRAPHIE BULLOZ)

The guillotine was not a wholly new invention, however. In this early woodcut, Aldegraver had depicted the Roman Titus Manlius beheading his son—with an early version of the guillotine (METROPOLITAN MUSEUM OF ART, GIFT OF HARRY G. FRIEDMAN, 1957)

Fouquier-Tinville, Public Prosecutor under the Terror, who gave Charles-Henri Sanson his orders each morning as to which prisoners were to be executed (BIBLIOTHEQUE NATIONALE)

A more florid engraving of Louis XVI in his last days (BIBLIOTHEQUE NATIONALE)

The first guillotine, erected on the place du Carousel, August 13, 1792, "to punish conspirators and enemies of the State" (METROPOLITAN MUSEUM OF ART, WHITTELSEY FUND, 1962)

Guillotine, élevée en Place du Carousel, le 13 aoust 1792. Servant à punir les conspirateurs et ennemis de la Patrie.

A Paris, chez Villion et Valmont, Md. d'Estampes et fabriquants de papier en rouleau, rue St. Jacques, à la Ville de Rouen. N° 8.

The Royal Family at play in the garden of the Temple Prison
(PHOTOGRAPHIE BULLOZ)

These two "versions" of Louis XVI's execution, each depicting a
different background, give some idea of the haste with which contemporary French artists tried to supply pictures of an event that
had fired the public imagination. The print above is captioned with
the King's alleged last words, the one below with a ballad, "Lament
on the Death of Louis XVI," in which the King recounts his crimes,
his imprisonment, and death in impeccable stanzas (PHOTOGRAPHIE
BULLOZ; METROPOLITAN MUSEUM OF ART, WHITTELSEY FUND, 1962)

COMPLAINTE SUR LA MORT DE LOUIS LE DERNIER.

Marie-Anne Charlotte Corday D'Armant, guillotined for the assassination of Jean-Paul Marat in 1793 (BIBLIOTHEQUE NATIONALE)

Louis XVI attempting to address the populace from the scaffold, from a contemporary print published in London (METROPOLITAN MUSEUM OF ART, WHITTELSEY FUND, 1962)

Marie Antoinette on her way to the guillotine, escorted by the National Guard. Another sketch of her, by Jacques-Louis David, shows the former Queen bareheaded and with her hands tied behind her, indicating that this engraving may have been conjectural (PHOTOGRAPHIE BULLOZ)

Journée du 16 Octobre 1793.

Marie Antoinette on the scaffold. J. S. Helman after C. Monnet

Madame Roland, whose courage on the way to the guillotine and eloquent last words drew hushed respect from the populace (PHOTOGRAPHIE BULLOZ)

Danton, arrested under the Terror, sketched by a contemporary artist en route to his execution (PHOTOGRAPHIE BULLOZ)

Maximilien Robespierre, "The Incorruptible" (BIBLIOTHEQUE NATIONALE)

This English conception of the death of Robespierre does not depict the injuries "The Incorruptible" suffered in trying to escape arrest (PHOTOGRAPHIE BULLOZ)

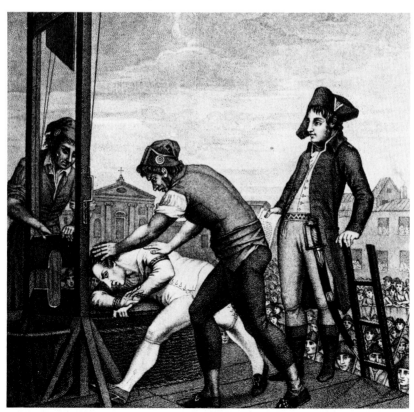

A cartoon of Charles-Henri Sanson. Under a banner reading "Robespierre's Government," he has apparently no more victims to decapitate and has nothing to do but guillotine himself (PHOTOGRAPHIE BULLOZ)

Grave Number 27 in the cemetery of Montmarte, where Henri-Clement, the last Sanson to hold the position of Executioner, lies buried (KENNETH H. STRAUS)

Vive la Guillotine
Qui fait si bonne mine
Et qui coupe si bien
Le cou à tous les chiens

Mes beaux aristocrates
Dans le sac à Sanson
Crachons, crachons.

Tomorrow Sanson, naively,
Will tell me: I must shave [off heads]
If you like, you can terrorize
The King in the other world.

I would buy some heads
If I had the means
I'd carry them in celebrations,
One in each hand.

Long live the Guillotine
Who has such a pleasant face
And who cuts so well
All the dogs' necks

My handsome aristocrats
In Sanson's sack
Let's spit, let's spit.

"The Guillotine, we find," said *Thomas*
Carlyle, "gets always a quicker motion, as other things
are quickening. The Guillotine, by its speed of going, will
give index of the general velocity of the Republic. The

[135]

clanking of its huge axe, rising and falling there, in horrid systole-diastole, is portion of the whole enormous life-movement and pulsation of the Sansculottic System!"

After the Queen's trial came that of the inhabitants of Armentières, charged with conspiracy with the enemy; six men were exonerated, four sentenced to death and executed. On the 1st of Brumaire (October 22nd) came Louis Armand Pernon, manager of the National Pottery, accused of having corresponded with the rebels of Lyon; on the 2nd of Brumaire, Pierre Hippolyte Pastourel, a priest. On the 3rd of Brumaire the Girondins appeared before the Tribunal and were found guilty of conspiring against the unity and indivisibility of the Republic. On the 10th of Brumaire, twenty-one of them mounted the scaffold and went to their death.

On the 16th of Brumaire, the guillotine claimed one of its most famous and infamous victims. Louis-Philippe-Joseph, duc d'Orléans, Prince of the Blood, and reputedly the richest man in France, had been one of the early supporters of the Revolution, currying favor with the populace, flattering its leaders, and going so far as to change his name to Philippe Égalité—a thoroughly disgraceful and cowardly move for a member of the royal family. Hated by the royalists, he became an embarrassment and a threat to the revolutionaries, who were never sure of his loyalty, despite the odious fact that he had voted for the death of his cousin, Louis XVI. To everyone's surprise, he went to his death bravely, even haughtily, with a smile on his lips.

> At three o'clock, [writes Lamartine,] "they came to get him for the ride to the scaffold. Prisoners in the Conciergerie, almost all of whom

despised not only his role in the Revolution but
the very name of the duc d'Orléans, thronged the
corridors and the courtyards to see him pass. He
was escorted by six gendarmes, their swords
unsheathed. His bearing, his attitude, his
expression, the briskness of his footsteps on the
flagstones were more those of a soldier marching
into battle than those of a condemned man being
taken to the scaffold. The Abbé Lothringer
climbed into the tumbrel with him . . . squadrons
of mounted gendarmes formed an escort. The
tumbrel moved slowly. Every eye was on the
Prince, some vengefully, others as if in atonement.

Clad in a blue dress coat, a white pique vest, and
leather culottes, his boots were polished to a high gloss,
and he was as coiffed and powdered as if going to a
palace ball. At the scaffold, he exhibited an incredible
sang-froid. When one of the aides wanted to remove his
boots which were tight-fitting and narrow, he smiled.
"They'll be much easier to remove afterward."

But Philippe Égalité had no monopoly on courage.
Jeanne Manon Phlipon Roland de la Platière, whose
salon was the intellectual gathering place for the Girondists, was accused and found guilty of having participated
in "a horrible conspiracy against the unity, the indivisibility of the Republic, the liberty and the safety of the
French people." This brave woman, whose husband had
been Inspector General of Commerce in Rouen and
Amiens, and in 1792 Minister of the Interior, followed
her friends to the guillotine on the 18th Brumaire
(November 8th). Riouffe, who was with her in prison, left
a poignant description of her last hours:

The day of her condemnation, she was clad in
white; her long black hair hung to her waist; her

[137]

appearance would have melted the hardest of hearts, but did those monsters [the tribunal] have hearts to melt? After her condemnation she returned with a lightness of step that was almost joyous; she lifted a finger to let us know that she was doomed. Married to a man for whom the same fate was in store, but whose courage did not equal hers, she managed to show him what bravery could be, and with such true gaiety and gentleness that she brought a smile to his lips.

(Accused of royalism, her husband fled Paris. When he learned that his wife had been executed, he committed suicide.)

Madame Roland's ride to the scaffold was a strange one. The mob, which usually indicated its thirst for blood, fell strangely silent as she passed. A contemporary account says that from time to time there were a few shouts from those paid to insult victims en route to the guillotine, but for the most part, men and women looked upon this dignified woman with pity in their hearts. At one point, shouts of "To the Guillotine, to the Guillotine" were heard, and Madame Roland smiled. "I'm going," she replied. "Soon I'll be there. And those who have sent me will not be long in following. I go to my death innocent, they will go as criminals; and you will applaud them, as you are now applauding me." A man named Lamarche, who had been condemned at the same time as Madame Roland, rode to the scaffold with her. Noticing the man's ashen pallor and violent trembling, she turned to him, saying: "You may precede me; at least I can spare you the pain and suffering of seeing my blood."

Charles-Henri, whose orders from Fouquier-Tinville included the order of precedence, had been instructed to guillotine Madame Roland first, and consequently demurred; whereupon the intrepid woman gave him a sad smile. "Surely you will not refuse a woman her last request," she said. Charles-Henri, whose distress was far greater than his victim's, acceded, his only desire to blot the entire picture from sight and memory.

But the executioner's memory, no less than the history of France, would be emblazoned with Madame Roland's words as she mounted the scaffold. Catching sight of the statue of liberty, she spoke the now famous line: *O liberté, liberté, comme on t'a jouée!* (Literally, "Oh liberty, liberty, how they have played with you!" but more dramatically expressed by Lamartine in his *History of the Girondins*, "Oh liberty, what crimes are committed in thy name!")

Three days later, Jean-Sylvain Bailly, first President of the Constituent Assembly, first mayor of Paris, and distinguished astronomer, went to his death for the sin of royalism. A cold November rain drenched the Parisian populace lining the route of the tumbrels, hurling insults and mud at its latest victim. Charles-Henri, whose soft-heartedness was known to many, gazed sorrowfully at his prisoner, then suggested that because of the inclement weather, it might be wise for Bailly to put his coat on. The response, which failed to amuse the executioner, was accompanied by a bitter laugh. "What's the matter? Are you afraid I might catch cold?"

The toll of victims mounted: fifty-one in October, fifty-eight in November, sixty-eight in December, of whom sixteen were women—among the latter, a figure from Charles-Henri's past. In her fifties now, her skin blotched, her waistline thickened, the executioner describes his shock upon seeing her again. "It had been twenty years or more since I had seen her, and I wouldn't have recognized her, so disfigured had she become by embonpoint, by sorrow, and by anguish."

Jeanne Bécu Gomard de Vaubernier, comtesse du Barry, had made the sad mistake of returning from London. As the mistress of the late Louis XV, she was immediately "suspect" and she had compounded the felony by having furnished financial aid to emigres. When the executioner went to the Conciergerie for her, he found her frenzied with fear:

> Her teeth were chattering, her voice came from her throat; hoarse, gasping. Like many others, I was moved to tears, but my tears were more bitter than the rest, for the sight of this unhappy woman brought back my youth, in which there was no thought of a destiny such as this. In spite of all my efforts to control my emotions, never had a journey seemed so long.

It took three men to hold her so that her hands could be bound and her hair cut; Charles-Henri turned away from the sight of the terrified woman, who wrestled with his aides, screaming that she was innocent, and pleading that they save her from death. The journey that seemed interminable to Charles-Henri ended at last, and the screams turned to sobs. "No, no, it can't be. You're not going to let me die," she gasped. Charles-Henri, overcome by emotion, walked away from her, signaling his son to perform the task that he himself could not face.

Madame Louise-Elizabeth Vigée-Lebrun, the well-known artist who had painted three portraits of Madame du Barry, mentions the execution in her *Souvenirs*:

> Arrested, put in prison, Madame du Barry was judged and condemned to death by the

[140]

revolutionary tribunal at the end of 1793. She is
the only woman, among all the women who
perished during the dreadful days, who could not
stand the sight of the scaffold. She screamed, she
begged mercy of the horrible crowd that stood
around the scaffold, she aroused them to such a
point that the executioner grew anxious and
hastened to complete his task. This convinced me
that if the victims of these terrible times had not
been so proud, had not met death with such
courage, the terror would have ended much
earlier. Men of limited intelligence lack the
imagination to be touched by inner suffering, and
the populace is more easily stirred by pity than by
admiration.

Charles-Henri would have been the first to agree with
Madame Vigée-Lebrun, knowing that his own suffering
was shared increasingly by the people of Paris.

An interesting sequel to the execution of Madame du
Barry is reported in *Anecdotes secrètes de la Terreur*, with the
dateline 17 Frimaire, an II (December 7, 1793):

Cemetery of the Madeleine . . . a man was
waiting, dressed in bottle-green . . . suddenly the
rumble of a cart was heard. It stopped and three
men pulled a heavy object from the straw. A
smaller object was handed to the waiting man. It
was a decapitated head, upon which drops of
blood had become clotted and tangled in a mass
of ash-blonde hair as curly as that of a child. The
man took the head, and from beneath his cloak he
drew forth a lump of soft wax, oil, brushes.
Placing the head on the ground, he knelt in front
of it and began to model. Because of this work,

[141]

Curtius, director of the Wax Museum, was able to exhibit in his collection the authentic portrait of Jeanne Gomard de Vaubernier, comtesse du Barry. It was her decapitated head that Sanson's tumbrel had just deposited in the cemetery.

John Christopher Curtius was the uncle of Marie Grosholtz, better known to history as Madame Tussaud.

The Sanson family's relationship with the future Madame Tussaud began with the Revolution. Although Marie-Anne Jugier Sanson and the young Marie Grosholtz enjoyed a personal friendship, the principal reason for the liaison between families was one of business. Pursued by financial worries throughout the revolutionary years, Charles-Henri had to look beyond his official job for ways of earning money. His neighbors might traffic in salt, sugar, or soap (a black market existed in many commodities) but the executioner had other means at his disposal. We know he sold cadavers to surgeons, and Mercier tells us that he also sold a remedy against rheumatism, which he concocted from the *graisse de pendu* (fat of his victims). His meeting with John Christopher Curtius provided him with an added resource, the renting of heads for the modeling of death masks and busts.

Curtius, a native of Berne, had left Switzerland and

emigrated to Strasbourg in 1760. He had given up the practice of medicine, but his interest in science, plus great manual dexterity made him turn to modeling parts of the human anatomy in wax. He managed to procure the necessary organs and limbs from hospitals and morgues, reproduced them, and sold them to medical schools, to surgeons, and to hospitals. Then, learning that families often wanted likenesses of their loved ones, he began making masks. One of his trips to Paris resulted in a chance encounter with the prince de Conti, whose enthusiasm for the wax portraits convinced Curtius that the capital city might prove to be a more profitable home for his talents.

His sister had married a military man named Grosholtz and had been recently widowed, and inasmuch as she was without means, he brought her and her six-year-old daughter Marie to Paris to live with him. He opened a small gallery in the rue Saint-Honoré where he exhibited busts of famous men of the day, admitting the public for a small fee. Gradually his studio became a rendezvous for artists and writers, for philosophers and poets and courtiers: such men as Voltaire, Rousseau, La Fayette, Mirabeau, and Benjamin Franklin frequented his workshop. It is said that Franklin became fascinated with the procedure and commissioned a portrait of himself. The success of his venture encouraged the clever Curtius to go a step further. Instead of limiting his modeling to face and head, he decided to model the entire figure, dress it appropriately, and place it in a setting, thereby creating a *tableau vivant*. These little scenes were greeted with such enthusiasm that he moved to larger quarters at 20 boulevard du Temple and his erstwhile gallery became a museum.

Here, figures of royal blood and men of letters were

joined by a so-called *Caverne des Voleurs,* forerunner of the present-day chamber of horrors at the waxworks in London. He modeled the figures of thieves and cut-throats in the act of performing their robberies and murders, he showed victims undergoing torture on the wheel and hanging from the gallows, and he showed the executioner wielding his axe. In need of expert advice on such activity, it was quite logical for him to seek out the man whose knowledge would be the most accurate and the most extensive—Charles-Henri Sanson.

Young Marie Grosholtz exhibited a strong talent for her uncle's profession, quickly becoming adept at modeling the flowers and fruit so much in vogue among the aristocracy and rich bourgeois as table decor or ornamentation in salons. Her skill at portraiture also developed to such a point that the King's sister, Madame Elizabeth, who was a frequent visitor at Curtius's atelier, persuaded Marie to live at Versailles and teach her the art. Marie spent several years at the royal palace, while her uncle continued to enlarge his exhibits and his circle of acquaintances.

In 1789, Curtius—at heart a royalist, but one who suddenly deemed it wise to espouse republicanism—summoned his niece from Versailles. Having volunteered for the attack on the Bastille, he undoubtedly feared for Marie's safety if she remained with the royal family; he also needed her services. She arrived home on July 12th, just two days before the siege, and joined him at the prison, where she took casts of the faces of the comte de Lorge (who had been a prisoner for over thirty years) and of the marquis de Launay, governor of the Bastille. In her memoirs, she tells the story of visiting the dungeons. While descending the narrow stairway, her foot slipped. She was saved from falling by a young man named

Maximilien Robespierre, who remarked that it would have been a pity to have so young and pretty a woman break her neck in such a horrid place. A few years later she would hold his severed head in her lap in order to make his death mask.

Marie Grosholtz would mold likenesses of Charlotte Corday, of Marie Antoinette, of Marat and Necker and Philippe d'Orléans. As the Revolution quickened, the simplest and most efficient means of obtaining heads for her portraiture was to deal directly with Charles-Henri Sanson. At night, his tumbrels deposited the guillotined heads with her, returning the following morning to collect them for burial. All "enemies of the people" were molded in wax, and crowds lined up outside the museum to view the latest portrait.

It was inevitable that Marie's friendship with Madame Elizabeth and her long stay at Versailles should make her "suspect." The fact that she was growing rich on the proceeds of the wax museum added to the Revolutionary Tribunal's eagerness to accuse her. She was arrested and imprisoned in the La Force prison, where she claims to have shared a cell with Josephine de Beauharnais, future Empress of France. No one knows who interceded for her, but it must have been someone in a position of power, because after a three-month stay she was released and permitted to resume her life. Soon afterward, her uncle's death made her sole heir to the museum and to a considerable fortune.

In 1795 she married François Tussaud, an engineer from Mâcon who was eight years her junior. Although they had two sons and a daughter, the marriage was not a congenial one, and in 1802 Marie left for England, taking with her her oldest son as well as the great part of the exhibition. François stayed in Paris to manage a

[145]

smaller collection, but gambling debts forced him to mortgage and subsequently lose it. The other children then joined their mother in London.

Madame Tussaud's waxworks, famous the world over, began as a traveling exhibit, but in 1834, tired of journeying from one town to another, Marie Tussaud settled the exhibition in Baker Street, where she continued to mold portraits until the age of eighty-one. She died in 1850 at the age of ninety, her career and her fame due in no small measure to her liaison with Charles-Henri Sanson.

In 1854, Charles-Henri's grandson Henri-Clément is supposed to have sold the blade of the guillotine to Marie's son, Joseph Tussaud, but as the original London waxworks and its records burned in 1925, there is no proof of this transaction.

Charles-Henri's loathing for the Revolu-tion and the machinations of its blood-soaked leaders increased with every passing day. But he admitted, albeit sardonically, that in one respect it had helped him and his confrères. "The Republic treated us better than the Monarchy," he said. "It was without doubt the only epoch in which the disgrace and public censure of our profession disappeared almost completely. In place of the insurmountable aversion we had always inspired, during the Terror we became aware that representatives of the people, orators from the revolutionary clubs who were known for their good citizenship, and the flower of the *sans-culottes* considered it an honor to fraternize with the executioner. Liberty, Equality, Fraternity, and Death!"

Those who knew the executioner personally or by sight, hailed him in the streets, saying: "Here's Charlot" or "There goes Sans-farine"; but the greetings were friendly, the sobriquets no more malicious than "Pierrot" or "Jeannot" or any other diminutive. Sanson had become a person of importance, a man to be respected as well as feared. It was even proposed that he be given the title of *Vengeur du Peuple* (avenger of the people) and that he dress in special clothing so that the entire nation should be aware of his importance. Jacques-Louis David, famed artist and member of the Convention, was fired with enthusiasm for the idea and designed a costume modeled on that of the lictors of ancient Rome. He went to call upon Charles-Henri and showed him the sketch, expecting praise and enthusiasm for his effort; but the executioner rebelled, refusing to change his dark green redingote and tricorn hat for any such nonsense. After all, he had spent a lifetime trying to look and act and live as other men; he had no desire to do anything that would underline or stress the difference.

The Terror gathered momentum. According to the estimate of Robert Christophe in his work on the Sansons, from the creation of the Revolutionary Tribunal on March 11, 1793, to the 9th of Thermidor (July 27, 1794), Charles-Henri, his aides, and members of his family escorted 1,256 people to the scaffold on the place de la Révolution. At the place de la Bastille and the place du Trône Renversé (other localities where the guillotine operated at various times) they executed 1,376

[147]

victims. In all, the Sanson family—father, son, and brothers—guillotined 2,362 people in 502 days.

And the Terror reigned the length and breadth of France. To enforce it, replicas of the Revolutionary Tribunal in Paris were set up in the provinces, where deaths were estimated at 20,000. In the Vendée, where civil war still raged, the republicans set out to teach the rebellious population a harsh lesson. Nantes, the center of unrest, was filled with so many prisoners that the prisons couldn't hold them. The guillotine, considered too slow a method of execution for such vast numbers, was discarded in favor of "fusillades" in which thousands were shot, and "noyades" or mass drownings in the Loire river. Men, women, and children perished in an excess of revolutionary zeal and brutality unequaled anywhere in France.

Among the men responsible for this horror was a provincial lawyer named Carrier, who would be recalled to Paris in February 1794 and guillotined during the days following the fall of Robespierre. Similar extermination of "enemies of the people" went on in Lyon, Toulon, Marseille, Bordeaux, and many other cities and towns. Gone and forgotten were the ideas of enlightenment promised by the Revolution; forgotten, too, were its humane principles. Tyranny prevailed.

And marching hand in glove with tyranny went famine. Civil war in the French colony of Santo Domingo resulted in a scarcity of sugar. Coffee was in short supply, as were oil, soap, salt, butter, eggs, and grain. Inflation made the peasants unwilling to exchange their meat and vegetables for the worthless paper currency called *assignats*. To add to the distress, wages remained the same while food prices soared. Several attempts at price-fixing by the government were unsuccessful, and a black market thrived in all commodities.

Danton, who had believed in the Terror at its outset, now found himself sickened by it. Not only had the policies of the "Montagne" increased in violence, but its power had spread; it controlled the Convention, the Commune of Paris, the Jacobin Club, and the Committee of Public Safety. While Danton and others cried for justice and clemency from their seats in the Convention, his friend Camille Desmoulins in his journal *Le Vieux Cordelier* wrote a series of columns advocating the abandonment of Terror and a return to a sane, humane method of government. The articles, far more than the oratory, gave hope to a vast multitude tired of seeing friends and relatives go to the guillotine for nothing more than a whisper of discontent. Robespierre and his Committee of Public Safety could not tolerate such opposition.

Charles-Henri's own words tell the story:

> Citizens Danton, Camille Desmoulins, Lacroix, and Philippeaux were arrested and taken to the Luxembourg. . . . The attitude of the four proscribed men was very different; Camille looked gloomy, sad, beaten; Lacroix was equally dejected; Philippeaux looked calm, resigned; but Danton, probably to hearten and encourage the others, affected a stoic gaiety. . . . During the night of the 12th or 13th, the accused were transferred from the Luxembourg to the Conciergerie. The 13th of Germinal [April 2nd] they appeared before the Tribunal.
>
> To questions concerning his name and address, Danton replied: "I am Danton, quite well-known

to the Revolution. My abode will soon be that of nothingness, but my name will live in the Pantheon of history." When his turn came, Camille said: "I am thirty-three years old, a dangerous age for revolutionaries, the same age as the sans-culotte Jesus when he died."

Sixteen Dantonists went on trial, a trial which lasted from April 2nd to April 5th and which produced the customary travesty of justice, the accused being permitted neither counsel nor witnesses. All were found guilty of "conspiring to reestablish the monarchy, to destroy the Convention and the government of the Republic." They were sentenced on April 5th and executed the same day.

Charles-Henri concludes the story:

> Danton remained the same, right up to the guillotine, passing without transition from a state of violent anger to one of utter serenity. When we reached our destination, he saw the scaffold; his face paled and I noticed that his eyes were wet. My close scrutiny must have displeased him because he jabbed me with his elbow. His voice sounded angry. "Have you no wife, no children?" I answered that yes, I had a wife and children, whereupon he said: "I too, and thinking of them I become a man again." He lowered his head and I heard him murmur: "My beloved wife [who was pregnant], I shall not see you again; my child, I shall never see you."

His last words to Charles-Henri were: "Show my head to the people. It's worth looking at."

When Desmoulins mounted the scaffold, the execu-

[150]

tioner must have harbored a few bitter thoughts, remembering that this was the man who had penned the words *J'appelle un chat un chat, et Sanson le bourreau.* But Charles-Henri, knowing that Desmoulins' wife Lucile had been arrested the night before, felt more pity than anger. And when the condemned man held out a locket containing a piece of his wife's hair and asked the executioner to take it to Lucile's father, Charles-Henri promised to carry out his wishes.

True to his promise, the executioner went to the house of Monsieur Duplessis, Lucile's father. He was invited to come in, but not wishing to identify himself, he refused, only to have several passers-by stop and stare at him. Fearing that someone might recognize him, a reluctant Charles-Henri followed Duplessis into the house. No sooner had he sat down when he heard the sound of a baby crying in an adjoining room.

Duplessis excused himself and disappeared, only to come back a few moments later with the baby in his arms. "It is their son," he said, then looked at Charles-Henri. "You were there? You saw him?" Charles-Henri nodded, informing the bereaved father-in-law that Desmoulins' last words were for his loved ones. "And my poor daughter, my poor Lucile," said the distraught Duplessis. "Will they be as pitiless toward her? Will she be less fortunate than Camille? Will there be no one but the miserable *bourreau* to bring me news of her last words?" Before Charles-Henri could reply, a woman entered the room. It was Madame Duplessis, bringing the news that Lucile had to appear before the tribunal in two days.

Profoundly shocked and terrified that Madame Duplessis might recognize him as the man who had taken her son-in-law's life—and who would in all likelihood

[151]

take her daughter's as well—Charles-Henri admitted: "I took to my heels as if I had committed a crime."

Three days later, the twenty-three-year-old Lucile went to the guillotine. The executioner, overcome by the tragedy, saved some of her hair, wrapped it up, and choosing a stranger to carry out his errand, bade him take the package to Duplessis. Charles-Henri Sanson was no less worried about Duplessis's knowing his identity than he was about revealing his kindness, a quality inappropriate to his position.

"It must be admitted," writes the Abbé Carrichon in reference to the execution of the maréchale de Noailles, "either because of humane traits or because of a desire to finish quickly, that the execution was alleviated by the promptness and the dispatch of the executioner, and by the care with which he ordered all the condemned to stand with their backs to the scaffold so that they could not see anything."

Charles-Henri's deeds were noted, although his motives were suspect, or more frequently, misinterpreted by all of his contemporaries.

In May, Elizabeth, sister of Louis XVI, went to the guillotine, and in the days to come, the famed chemist Antoine Lavoisier, the actress Maria Grandmaison, and her eighteen-year-old servant Nicole Bouchard trod the same path. No class of society, no business or profession, no age group was immune. "Systole, diastole, swift and ever swifter goes the Axe of Samson," said Thomas Carlyle. ". . . If no speakable charge exist against a man, or Batch of men, Fouquier has always this: a Plot in the Prison. Swift and ever swifter goes Samson; up, finally to threescore and more at a Batch. It is the highday of Death: none but the Dead return not."

On October 24, 1793, the new Revolu-
tionary Calendar was adopted to supersede the Christian
calendar and to rid the minds of men of religious ideas
associated with it. The scientific part of it was mainly the
work of astronomers and mathematicians, its nomencla-
ture the creation of the poet Philippe Fabre d'Eglantine.

The "French Era" was to succeed the "Christian Era,"
now declared abolished. The years were to date not from
the birth of Christ, but from the birth of the French
Republic—September 22, 1792. The Year One, then,
ran from September 22, 1792, to midnight September 21,
1793. (The years 1789 to 1792 were not worthy of
belonging to the new era, being years of slavery under a
monarch.) The year would continue to have twelve
months, but all the months would be equal—this being
an era of equality—and were to consist of thirty days
each.

The five days at the end of the year were to belong to
no month, but were to be holidays, and would be given
special names, as would the sixth day in a leap year.

The months were given poetic names, descriptive of
the temperature or of processes of nature characteristic of
them. They were grouped in blocks of three, differen-
tiated from each other by the word terminations:

Vendémiaire   Month of the Vintage (September 22 to
October 21)

[153]

Brumaire	Month of Fogs (October 22 to November 21)
Frimaire	Month of Frosts (November 21 to December 21)
Nivôse	Month of Snow (December 21 to January 20)
Pluviôse	Month of Rains (January 20 to February 19)
Ventôse	Month of Winds (February 19 to March 21)
Germinal	The month of budding (March 21 to April 20)
Floréal	The month of flowering (April 20 to May 20)
Prairial	Meadowy month, or month when crops ripened (May 20 to June 19)
Messidor	The month of harvests (June 19 to July 19)
Thermidor	The month of heat (July 19 to August 18)
Fructidor	The month of Fruit, of harvests (August 18 through September 16)

The new calendar also abolished the week. The month was divided into three *décades* or periods of ten days.

The names of the Christian calendar—Sunday, Monday, Tuesday, etc.—were abolished in favor of ordinal numbers; thus the days of the *décade:*

> *Primidi, duodi, tridi, quartidi, quintidi,*
> *sextidi, septidi, octidi, monidi, décadi.*

The last day of the decade was known as *décadi* and was designated as a day of rest. One object of this change was to get men to forget Sunday and the days of religious festivals.

[154]

The month of Prairial (or May-June) of the year II (or 1794) of the Republic, "one and indivisible" is best described by a series of notes in the Sanson *Mémoires*:

> *9 Prairial.* Yesterday and today, the Conciergerie received fifty new prisoners. Fourteen men were executed today, all poor people and peasants from the country.
>
> *11 Prairial.* The tribunal does not sit on *décadi.* Despite the law that says all those condemned by the revolutionary tribunal shall be executed within twenty-four hours, those arrested in the afternoon of *nonidi* will live until *primidi.*
>
> *12 Prairial.* Thirteen condemned today.
>
> *14 Prairial.* The populace is growing more and more disgusted by this butchery. . . . Yesterday there were cries of "enough" and today, after the second execution, a whistle of disapproval came from the crowd.
>
> *17 Prairial.* Citizen Robespierre was for the second time, and unanimously reelected President of the Convention.
>
> *21 Prairial.* The Festival of the Supreme Being took place yesterday. . . . After four o'clock in the afternoon, the blade [of the guillotine] fell twenty-two times.

[155]

The overthrow of the Dantonists had left the "Incorruptible" Maximilien Robespierre triumphant in the Convention. Ambitious and tremendously powerful, he was the idol of the *sans-culottes,* radical revolutionaries, to whom he personified a new and glorious France. The Festival of the Supreme Being mentioned by Charles-Henri was one of two significant events that occurred within days of each other, the first delighting the populace, the second dashing its hopes.

The Revolutionary Calendar, which abolished Sundays and Saints' days, was used by everyone, as witness Charles-Henri's notes. But although Robespierre opposed Catholicism, he was not an atheist. He disapproved of the philosophy of Reason just as vigorously as he opposed the church of the *ancien régime,* believing, as did Rousseau, in religion's power to unify a people. He acknowledged the existence of a Supreme Being; he even decreed that "The French people recognize the existence of God and the immortality of the soul," but the traditional religion did not suit his purpose. Instead he created a revolutionary creed which in essence was that of patriotism, worship of country. He also decreed that ceremonies would be held to celebrate Liberty, Equality, Fraternity, the first to take place on June 8th, honoring the Supreme Being and inaugurating the new religion. Thereafter, there would be four a year, celebrating the attack on the Bastille (July 14th), the overthrow of the monarchy (August 10th), the execution of the "tyrant" Louis XVI (January 21st), and the execution of the Girondists (May 31st). The organization and execution of the June 8th spectacle were given to Jacques-Louis David, the much-honored artist and painter, and of course the starring role would belong to Robespierre, high priest of the new cult. There were processions and speeches. A statue of Atheism was set afire, and from its ashes emerged the figure of Wisdom;

there were hymns sung and the public, believing that a new era of peace would be theirs, shouted "Long live the Republic!"

Two days later, the dread law of the 22nd Prairial was introduced in the Convention, a law that provided for the reorganization of the Tribunal in order to increase its efficiency. The Tribunal would now be divided into four sections. The number of the jury required to convict was reduced, and only seven of the nine-member jury needed to be present. Even more than before, the Tribunal was for the purpose of punishing enemies of the people, and an enemy of the people was almost anyone who opened his mouth. Any evidence, no matter how slight, could send a man to the guillotine, and the accused was denied right to counsel. But the most important part of the law gave the Committee of Public Safety the power to send anyone before the Revolutionary Tribunal independently of the Convention—which meant that even members of the Convention itself could be accused and arrested. This law enacted by Robespierre and his followers would boomerang and ultimately be the cause of their own downfall and death.

"From the 15 Messidor [June]," records Charles-Henri, "the number of victims never fell below thirty per day, sometimes it reached sixty. Every illustrious name of the monarchy was added to the roster of martyrs . . . but obscure, plebeian names were almost always in the majority on the funeral list." And, as if the sights and sounds and smells of death were not enough, Parisians could buy a journal entitled *La Guillotine*, the purpose of which was printed on its masthead:

> Complete and precise list, giving name, age, rank, and address of all conspirators who have been condemned to death by the Revolutionary

Tribunal, established in Paris by the law of
March 17, 1792, and by the Second Tribunal
established by the law of March 10, 1793, to judge
the enemies of the nation. Price: 15 sols;
obtainable in Paris at Citizen Marchand's,
Galerie Neuve du Palais Égalité; at Citizen
Berthe's, rue Honoré, opposite 41 rue Florentin;
at Citizen Channaud's, 17 rue Eloi near the
palace, and at all bookstalls and drapers' shops.

As the Terror neared its climax, the fifty-five-year-old executioner's disgust intensified; he felt tired in body and spirit, weighted down as much by the tragedies he had witnessed as by the demands upon his physical strength. And to add to his burdens, his son Henri had left him to join the National Guard.

Filled with patriotic zeal, the tall, powerful, twenty-seven-year-old Henri had begun his military service as a captain of artillery, later transferring to the gendarmerie, where he maintained the same rank. Attached to the Revolutionary Tribunal, he became part of the corps detailed to keep order at the Palais de Justice, at the prisons, and as escort to the tumbrels transporting victims to the guillotine. His patriotism entitled him to wear a handsome blue tunic and a black bicorn adorned with a red pompom, but fate and his commanding officer must have smiled ironically at the sight of the young soldier whose ambition had led him far from the scaffold, only to send him back along the same route. In the spring of 1794 Henri returned to the artillery with orders to take 150 men and put down a rebellion of the peasantry in Brie. But by the time he reached his destination, the revolt had been quelled and he was recalled to Paris, where he remained on inactive military service until 1795.

Deprived of his son's services, Charles-Henri's workload and expenses increased substantially. The longer his list of victims, the more manpower and equipment he needed. Instead of four assistants he had seven; instead of two tumbrels he often used as many as nine, the rental of extra carts costing him fifteen francs apiece, and five francs for each driver. He had to buy baskets to transport the corpses, new straps for the *bascule* because they wore out rapidly; bran, hay, nails, grease for the grooves that held the blade of the guillotine. Then there were tips for gravediggers, not to mention the salaries of his new aides. His request for an increase in salary and allowances fell upon deaf ears; the Convention had more important matters than the complaints of the executioner to occupy its time. He'd keep his job because he could get no other.

The carnage continued. On the 19th of Messidor (July 7th) Charles-Henri was ordered to guillotine the sixty-nine-year-old Abbé de Salignac-Fénélon, a man who had devoted the last years of his life to helping the chimney-sweeps of Paris, boys as young as five and six years old, many of them orphans and all of them poor. When the children heard of his condemnation, they flocked to the place du Trône Renversé. As the old man climbed up onto the scaffold, he caught sight of them and asked Charles-Henri if he might be permitted to bless them. The executioner untied his hands, then stood back while the Abbé made the sign of the cross. After the execution, Charles-Henri bowed his head, and to his surprise, not only the young chimneysweeps but many of the spectators followed his lead—proof that for the vast majority of the French people, no constitutional form of religion could ever succeed in replacing the Catholic church. Further proof came on the 29th of Messidor when sixteen Carmelite nuns went to the guillotine and were permitted to sing a hymn and then genuflect before their

[159]

Mother Superior. Neither Charles-Henri nor his aides made any attempt to hurry them, and the mob remained silent throughout the ceremony.

On the 7th of Thermidor, thirty-six prisoners from Saint-Lazare went to their death, among them the thirty-one-year-old poet André Chénier; on the following day fifty-five were executed, nineteen of them women.

The law of the 22nd of Prairial, responsible for the rapid pace of the guillotine, had also done its work in the Convention. All of the deputies knew that they were no longer immune from suspicion, arrest, and sentence of death, and they now feared for their own lives. Factions formed, jealousies abounded, fraternité had ceased to exist. The world of politics was struck by the same fear that had struck the populace—fear of the man who had created that fear, Maximilien Robespierre. On the 8th of Thermidor, he tried to rally the Convention by accusing his enemies within it. He tried to prove that the deputies had organized a conspiracy against the liberty of the people and that they had contrived a plot aimed at patriots such as himself. Gradually, ominously, relentlessly, the Convention turned against him. On the 9th of Thermidor his appearance was greeted with cries of "Down with the tyrant!" In vain did he appeal, his lips dry, his voice hoarse. The deputies sneered, and a derisive cry was heard: "The blood of Danton is choking him."

"You want to avenge Danton?" was his desperate reply. "You cowards, why didn't you defend him!"

The demand for Robespierre's arrest was not long in coming. Along with it, the Convention ordered the arrest of Couthon, Saint-Just, Lebas, Hanriot, and Augustin Robespierre, the "Incorruptible" Maximilien's brother. The guilty were taken to prison; but that night, the 9th of Thermidor, the Commune of Paris and the Jacobin Club ordered an insurrection to rid the Convention of its oppressors—hoping that if they rescued Robespierre and his friends from jail, he would lead them. They managed to have the prisoners released and the group convened on the second floor of the Hôtel de Ville. Meanwhile in the square below, armed supporters of the Commune confronted troops organized by the Convention. A band of men managed to cross the square and fight their way into the building; shots were fired on the second floor. In the ensuing tumult, Augustin Robespierre threw himself from a window, Lebas killed himself, Couthon was hurled down the staircase, Saint-Just taken prisoner, and Maximilien Robespierre himself was found with a fractured jaw. (Some reports claim that he was shot, but the concensus is that he tried to commit suicide.) He was carried to the hall of the Convention where, mangled and bloodied, he was thrown on a table, exposed to the insults and jeers of the victors, and then taken to the Conciergerie.

At four o'clock in the afternoon of the 10th of Thermidor (July 28, 1794) Maximilien Robespierre was delivered to Charles-Henri Sanson and marched across the courtyard to a waiting tumbrel. According to an eyewitness, "Just as the tumbrels got under way, a woman whose clothing showed her to be a member of the bourgeoisie clung to the cart at the risk of being crushed to death, crying 'Go, go to hell, villain; and go knowing that with you go the curses and the maledictions of every wife, every mother!' "

Mercier's account carries the event to its conclusion:

> Where shall I find the true colors with which to
> paint a picture of the public happiness that
> existed in the midst of this terrible spectacle, to
> describe the explosion of burning joy that spread

and resounded as far as the scaffold itself? His name, accompanied by curses, is in every mouth; they no longer call him the *incorruptible,* the *virtuous* Robespierre; the mask has fallen away. They execrate him, they blame him for every crime perpetrated by both committees [the Committee of General Security and the Committee of Public Safety], they surge forward from shops, boutiques, and windows. Rooftops are covered with people, thronged by a huge mob of spectators drawn from every class of society, all with only one desire, *to see Robespierre led to his death.*

Instead of sitting on a dictator's throne, he is half-sitting, half-lying in the tumbrel that also holds his accomplices, Couthon and Hanriot. The noise and tumult that accompanies him is composed of a thousand joyous cries and mutual congratulation. His head is enveloped in dirty bloodstained bandages; only half of his pale, ferocious face is visible. His mutilated, disfigured companions look less like criminals than wild beasts caught in a trap. Even the burning sun cannot deter the women from exposing the lilies and roses of their delicate cheeks to its rays; they want to see the executioner of these citizens. . . .

On the scaffold, the executioner, as if spurred by the public's hatred, roughly tears away the bandage covering his wounds; he [Robespierre] roars like a tiger; his lower jaw snaps off from the upper jaw and blood spurts out, changing this human head into the head of a monster, the most horrible sight imaginable. His two companions, no less hideous in their torn, bloodstained clothing, were the acolytes of this famous criminal, for whose suffering no one can summon a vestige of pity. . . . The crowd surged forward, so as not to miss witnessing the exact second when

his head would go beneath the blade, that blade
to which he himself had sent so many others. The
applause lasted more than fifteen minutes!
Twenty-two heads fell with his.

Barras, in his *Mémoires*, continues the tale:

> Because of the profound deference accorded me
> by Fouquier [Tinville], I saw the executioner
> approaching me respectfully and humbly, his hat
> in hand . . . the executioner himself, citizen
> Sanson. "Where shall we put the bodies, citizen
> representative?" he asks.
> "Throw them into the same grave as Capet," I
> answer testily. "Louis XVI was worth more than
> these men."
> The executioner's baskets were transported to
> the cemetery of the Madeleine and the bodies
> thrown into a ditch near the alleged tomb of
> Capet.

Charles-Henri must have made his usual arrangement
with Marie Grosholtz, the future Madame Tussaud,
because the morning after the execution an eager public
saw a wax replica of Robespierre's head reposing on a
white cushion in the museum.

In more than one account of Robespierre's death, the
executioner is accused of having torn the bandages from
the victim's face in a cruel manner. In the *Mémoires*,
Charles-Henri's grandson defends his grandfather, citing
a particular accusation: "Monsieur Louis Blanc writes on
page 265 of Volume X of his *History of the Revolution*:
'When Robespierre was on the scaffold, the executioner,

an impassioned royalist, tore the bandage from his wounds with a rough and barbaric gesture. . . .' I have no need to justify this accusation of royalism that Monsieur Louis Blanc levels at the memory of my grandfather. . . . Charles-Henri Sanson forgot his hatreds and thought only of easing the cruel agony of those whom the law had commanded him to execute." (It seems strange that the executioner's grandson should label the accusation one of "royalism" rather than one of "cruelty"; but perhaps he thought that in the mind of Louis Blanc, a socialist writer, either the two were synonymous, or the first was the more important one to refute.)

The death of Robespierre signaled the end of the Terror. The policies of the Convention moderated and became more conservative, the Jacobin Club was closed, and the Revolutionary Tribunal deprived of some of its powers. (It would be abolished in May of 1795.) But too many families had suffered to forget in a matter of weeks the injustices and the inhumanity of the revolutionary committees. Amid the exultation and the joy, another cry arose: "À bas la queue de Robespierre"—down with the followers of Robespierre. The populace demanded an eye for an eye, punishment for those who had punished. On December 16, 1794, Carrier, the provincial lawyer responsible for the "fusillades" and the "noyades" in Nantes, went to the guillotine; his death was followed by the deaths of Grandmaison and Pinard and Hermann, onetime president of the Revolutionary Tribunal, and by the death of the Public Prosecutor, Fouquier-Tinville himself.

When Fouquier was led to the scaffold, amid tumultuous applause, he turned to Charles-Henri. "Villain! I thought I would be sending you to the place you are taking me." Fixing the executioner with an icy stare, he added, "Inasmuch as they have condemned the prosecutor, I see no reason why they shouldn't condemn the executioner. One is as guilty as the other."

This statement must have sent shivers down the spine of Charles-Henri Sanson, for there could be no disputing its logic. Why the populace never demanded the head of its headsman remains an enigma to this day. It is equally strange that the executioner of Paris, one of the most conspicuous figures of the Revolution, should have remained one of the most anonymous. In drawings, paintings, and etchings of the period (and in many contemporary accounts, diaries, and memoirs) he is referred to as "the executioner," but he has neither name nor face. We are familiar with the features of Louis XVI and Marie Antoinette, Dr. Guillotin and Robespierre, Marat, Charlotte Corday, Danton, Fouquier-Tinville, and many others; but there is not one likeness of Charles-Henri Sanson in existence.

———

Many of the harsh revolutionary laws were abolished during the months following Thermidor (July), but the nation was in an economic crisis. Inflation worsened as the government continued to print *assignats,* its leaders deluding themselves that the staggering deficit could be cured by issuing more paper. In July, an *assignat* designated to be worth one hundred francs had an actual value of thirty-four, in December it was worth seventeen.

[165]

The harvest of 1794 was a meager one, and the winter as cold as the winter of 1789. The poor of Paris had neither wood nor coal, neither meat nor bread. In the small towns and villages the peasants hoarded their crops, just as they had done in previous years.

When the Terror ended, Charles-Henri Sanson had been present at, assisted at, directed, or actually performed over 2,700 executions. Unlike the rest of Paris, he had no further thirst for blood; he wanted only to escape and to forget. During this period of his life, he spent increasing amounts of time at Brie-Comte-Robert, digging in his garden, planting vegetables and flowers, and pruning his trees. But even there, disgust and disillusionment followed him. Witness the following comment, dated 13 Pluviôse, year II (December, 1794):

> I have just returned from Brie where our country house is located. The three days I spent there make me loath to return. The word "Fraternity" that glitters on the façade of the town hall is far from being engraved upon the hearts of men. The citizens of the countryside think only of money. The sale of public lands, far from satisfying them, merely increases their greed. The law is supposed to punish those who hoard; if that were true, we should need a guillotine in every village, because even the smallest farmer hides his wheat, fearing that he might be forced to take it to market and sell it for *assignats*. There are still revolutionary committees in the larger towns, but the peasants are thick as thieves; there is no danger of any man denouncing his neighbor. They have all formed an association which defies the orders of the Convention, and which is the underlying cause of famine.

There were outbreaks of violence and insurrections throughout the winter and spring of 1795; for as the American Minister, Gouverneur Morris, wrote to George Washington in December 1794, "The French are tired of war; they have only scorn and hatred for the present government, and in my opinion, would like nothing better than the restoration of the monarchy." The war was going well, partly because of compulsory military service, partly because of new, young commanders. They defeated the English and the Austrians, they recaptured Belgium and conquered Holland, they drove back the Spaniards and the Prussians. But the French people were paying for the war in terms of death and famine and misery, no small share of it caused by Frenchmen themselves.

In Paris the government changed, the Convention giving way to the Directoire, and in the field—specifically in the campaign being waged in northern Italy—a new general had taken command, a man whose military genius would be equaled if not excelled by his diplomatic and political ability: Napoleon Bonaparte.

On 13 Fructidor, year III (August 30, 1795), a tired Charles-Henri again resigned his office, stating in his letter of resignation that he had served as executioner for forty-three years, and that ill health, specifically nephritis ("Nephrétique"), made him unable to continue. He asked for a pension of one thousand francs a year. His resignation was accepted and on the 4th of September his son replaced him. Charles-Henri and his wife then retired to their house at Brie-Comte-Robert.

The Revolution had taken a frightful toll. A listing of the executions in Paris from July 14, 1789, to October 21, 1796, gives a sobering analysis of the kind of men the state had considered its enemies.

AGE	NUMBER
Under 18 years	22
18–20 years	45
20–25 years	336
25–50 years	1,669
50–60 years	528
60–70 years	206
70–80 years	103
Over 80 years	9
Men	2,518
Women	370
Sex unrecorded	30

PROFESSION AND RANK OF THOSE EXECUTED

Churchmen—Bishops and Archbishops	6
Marshals of France and Generals	25
Magistrates—Members of Parlement	246
Ecclesiastics—Monks, Friars	319
Members of the Assembly—	
Constituent and Legislative	39
Members of the Convention	45
Members of the Commune	72
Financiers, lawyers, doctors, notaries	479
Nobles of both sexes	381
Officers and soldiers	365
Men and women of letters	25
Artists	16
Merchants of both sexes	275
Artisans	391
Domestic servants—coachmen, gardeners	129
Laborers, farmers	105
	2,918

Emigrations before and during The Terror (approximate)

Priests	27,000
Military men of the nobility	8,400
Noblemen—nonmilitary	16,900
Men of Parlement	160
Men of law	2,800

Bankers and Financiers	240
Merchants	7,800
Notaries	210
Physicians and Surgeons	540
Landlords, men of property	9,900
Farmers	3,400
Seafarers of the nobility	2,000
Aristocrats—women	8,000
Nuns and Abbesses	4,400
Artisans	18,000
Wives of artisans	3,000
Domestic servants	2,800
Children of both sexes	3,100
Soldiers and sailors	900
TOTAL	119,550

A document dated 4 Pluviôse, year X (January 24, 1802), reveals that no pension had been forthcoming for Charles-Henri. In a letter written by the man in charge of public debt to the Minister of Justice, we learn that:

> Citizen Sanson, erstwhile executioner of criminal judgments, having retired, claims a pension for his services. Documents appended to his request reveal that he did not actually take office until February 1, 1778, and that he has not had the thirty years of service required by the law of August, 1790, in order to qualify for a pension. He states that he resigned because of illness, and for that reason he is entitled, by right of the same law, to be considered as having served thirty years.

No record survives; but it is doubtful that this second plea brought him any more satisfaction than the first.

For several years after his resignation, Charles-Henri continued to spend time in Paris, but rarely left his house except to visit the church of Saint-Laurent. One day in 1806, not long before his death, the sixty-seven-year-old executioner decided to go for a walk, choosing as his destination the site of the present-day Madeleine. Construction of a church begun in 1764 had been interrupted by the Revolution, and now Napoleon had ordered a temple built on that site, dedicated to the glory of his *Grande Armée*. Charles-Henri had just arrived when Napoleon appeared, followed by a large entourage. The executioner tried to back away, but before he could escape, one of Napoleon's aides recognized him and escorted him to the Emperor. Napoleon asked him why he was there, and then seeing a volume of Racine's poetry in the executioner's hand, he reached for it.

"Who are you?"

"Sire, I am Sanson, the executioner."

Napoleon threw the book to the ground. "Were you the executioner in 1793?"

"Yes, Sire."

"If, one day, there were an uprising against me . . . if anyone dared to—"

"Sire, I executed Louis XVI."

Napoleon paled visibly, then managed to recover his aplomb. "Pick up your book and get out of my sight," he said brusquely.

A record of this episode, found in the Sanson family papers, is supposedly authentic. True or not, it is fair to assume that any man who had survived the Revolution and the Terror could have no fear of any man—even an Emperor.

Sébastien Mercier, ever-fascinated by the *Bourreau de Paris*, expresses the curiosity and the speculation that has existed throughout history regarding Charles-Henri Sanson, *Le Grand*.

It is the executioner. Voltaire said that the executioner should write the history of the English. One might say the same of Sanson, that he should write the history of the Reign of Terror. . . . What a man is Sanson! Impassive, he is always one with the blade of death. . . . He chops off whatever head is brought to him. What an instrument, what a man! He must fear being alone for even one day in Paris. . . . What does he say? What does he think? I should like to know what goes on in his head, if he thinks of his terrible job as just a job. . . . He received the Queen's apology, so they say, when on the scaffold she accidentally trod on his foot. What were his thoughts? He was for many years paid by the Royal Treasury. What a man is Sanson! He comes and goes like everyone else; he occasionally attends the theater; he laughs, he looks at me; my head has eluded him, he knows nothing about it, and as he is indifferent to me, I shall not waste time pondering the indifference with which he has sent so many men of all ranks into the next world; he would begin again . . . and why not? Isn't it his job?

The Revolutionary Calendar was abolished on January 1, 1806. On July 4, Charles-Henri Sanson died in his house at number 10 rue Neuve Saint-Jean. A service was held in the church of Saint-Laurent and his body buried in the Cemetery of the North, which today is the cemetery of Montmartre. The simple stone is still there, surrounded by an iron grille, the chiseled letters faint but still legible:

CHARLES HENRY
SANSON
né à Paris
le 15 fevrier 1739
décédé le 4 juillet 1806

Cette pierre lui fut érigée
par son fils et sa famille
dont il fut regrette.

(This stone was erected to him
by his son and family
by whom he was regretted.)

On the 13th Vendémiare (October 5,
1795) a young Corsican artillery officer named Buona-
Parte succeeded in putting down an insurrection by the
Parisian populace, the first in a series of victories that
would ultimately win him the title of Emperor. On the
4th of September, one month before this uprising,
another young artillery officer named Henri Sanson
confronted his future and decided upon a course that
would also win him a title, that of *Monsieur de Paris.*

Young Henri, who had eschewed the scaffold to join
the *Garde Nationale* in the late autumn of 1793, experienced a rather alarming few days in the period following
the Terror. On the 9th of Thermidor he had received
orders from his commanding officer (orders emanating
from the Commune of Paris) to take his company to the
place de Grève. A few hours later, he and his uncle
Pierre-Charles Sanson—a lieutenant in the same com-

pany—had been transferred to the quai des Orfèvres, headquarters of the municipal police. Shortly after their arrival they watched Robespierre, escorted by two gendarmes, enter the Palais de Justice which adjoined police headquarters on the quai. Robespierre the Terrorist, a popular figure with the police, did not remain there long; a delegation from the Commune prevailed upon him to go to the Hôtel de Ville, where much to their surprise he was received with cheers and applause. By this time the two Sansons had surmised that events were not proceeding too well for the Commune, and concluded that if they were known to have been in the vicinity of police headquarters, their own position might be suspect. Anyone seen with or near Robespierre ran the risk of being tarred with the same brush. They returned to their section, thankful to have escaped from a dangerous area of the city.

Unfortunately their presence had been noted. On the 14th of Thermidor, they and the rest of their company were denounced and accused of having offered their services to Robespierre and his henchmen. Forty-three members of the company were arrested and sent to the Conciergerie, where it is said that Henri Sanson occupied the same cell in which Marie Antoinette had been confined for so long. Fortunately, however, the law of the 22nd Prairial had been abolished, and they were permitted to retain the services of a lawyer. Because of Charles-Henri's large acquaintance, the old executioner succeeded in hiring Claude Chauveau-Lagarde to plead his son's case. Chauveau-Largarde had defended Marie Antoinette, Charlotte Corday, and the King's sister, Madame Elizabeth, but now he was more successful: forty-two out of the forty-three were acquitted. The only man found guilty of treachery and sentenced to die was a certain Joseph-Julien Lemonnier, captain in the National Guard. Had Henri Sanson been convicted, his own father would have been ordered to execute him.

The young man had assisted his father during the beginning years of the Revolution, had lived through the Terror and been witness to its atrocities, and had narrowly escaped the guillotine himself. Small wonder that he should hesitate when it came time to choose between staying in the artillery or assuming what had become if not a hereditary position, then at least a tradition in the Sanson family. He personally recorded his father's advice to him on the subject of his future:

> It is your turn to take on the responsibility and trust that has belonged to our family. The post will bring you more than twelve thousand livres a year. You would be wise to take it, my boy. Because you must understand that the prejudice against us will always exist and prevent you from advancing in rank, it may even deprive you of the rank of captain. This way you will live in peace, and at least no one will have the right to meddle in your affairs.

It must have been a difficult decision to make, for being an officer in the National Guard meant that Henri enjoyed not only the privileges of rank, but what was for the Sanson family an extraordinary freedom. He could walk the streets of Paris and the provinces as a respected member of the community; he was considered a citizen not a pariah. But he had grown up in a household of executioners; he had listened to his uncles and his father speak of the trials and tribulations that confronted executioners when they tried to live and act as other men. He had experienced prejudice and been the victim

[174]

of insults himself. A realist? A fatalist? A coward? He may have been a little of each; he'd have been a fool if he had refused to recognize the truth in his father's words. And Henri Sanson was neither a fool nor a gambler. Better a guaranteed income than no income at all. He resigned his commission in the National Guard and in August of 1795 he succeeded his father as Monsieur de Paris.

A tall, vigorous, rather good looking man, he is depicted in most of the contemporary accounts as having the build of a Hercules. Despite a bald head (he lost his hair quite early in life), he had classic features and a wardrobe that marked him as a dandy. Grace Dalrymple Elliott, an Englishwoman confined in the Récollets prison in 1793, describes her first sight of him:

> I was much shocked one day, [she wrote,] on going into the gaoler's room, where we used sometimes to go when we wanted anything. He was sitting at a table with a very handsome, smart young man, drinking wine. The gaoler told me to sit down and drink a glass too. I did not dare to refuse. The young man then said, "Well, I must be off," and looked at his watch. The gaoler replied, "No; your work will not begin till twelve o'clock." I looked at the man, and the gaoler said to me, "You must make friends with this citizen; it is young Samson, the executioner, and perhaps it may fall his lot to behead you." I felt quite sick, especially when he took hold of my throat saying, "It will soon be off your neck, it is so long and small. If I am to despatch you, it will be nothing but a squeeze."

Mrs. Elliott, who regained her liberty after an eighteen-month stay in various prisons, quite obviously saw herself (in retrospect) as the heroine of all heroines. Her journal resembles nothing more than *The Perils of Pauline*; but despite her fears, she was not too terrorized to notice the "very handsome, smart young man." Henri was twenty-six years old when she saw him, on a day shortly before the death of Marie Antoinette, and a matter of weeks before he entered the National Guard.

His marriage must have taken place during the Revolution, because there is no record of it. (Either the nuptial mass was celebrated by a nonjuring priest, or there was only a civil ceremony.) In October of 1817, the union was sanctified in the church of Saint-Laurent. His bride, Marie-Louise Damidot, born October 14, 1776, belonged to a well-to-do family who were not part of the confrèrie of executioners—another departure for the Sansons. According to all reports, she was a beautiful woman, and a faithful and devoted wife. They had four children: Henri-Clément, the oldest son, born in 1799, would succeed his father; two girls, Marie-Gabrielle, born in 1802, and Adelaïde, born in 1804, both married executioners, the former wedding the executioner of Lyon, the latter that of Versailles. A fourth child, Nicolas-Eugène, born in 1810, was baptized in the church of Saint-Laurent as were all of the children, but of this second son nothing is known.

Like his forbears, Henri Sanson led a quiet, ordered life, preferring the company of his family to that of outsiders. During the first years of his marriage, he lived in the rue Saint-Jacques de la Boucherie in the *quartier* of Les Halles, but subsequently he moved into his father's house in the rue Neuve Saint-Jean. Sometime after 1818 he acquired a dwelling at 31 bis rue des Marais. As if the fact of living under his own roof indicated the necessity of a change, he settled into the mold of a solid, bourgeois *père de famille.* His main meal was served at one o'clock; at five he took a light repast known as *goûter*, and his supper was put on the table at eight. Afterward he enjoyed a game of piquet with his family. Unlike his predecessors, Henri did not permit his aides to become an integral part of the family; they lived in outbuildings on his land and entered his house morning and evening for prayers, but they did not act as house servants, confining their usefulness to the scaffold.

And with this move to the rue des Marais came a change in Henri's style of dress. From now until the end of his life he wore only black, affecting a lace jabot and a gold watch chain, the essence of solid respectability. His appearance during the reign of Louis-Philippe was so dignified and correct that it caused a contemporary to remark: "With his very proper air, anyone would take him for the mayor of a small town in the suburbs, on his way to officiate at a marriage ceremony. . . ." The Sanson family had come a long way from Abbeville and the sturdy boots and coarse woolens of their ancestor.

A kind man, Henri distributed bread to the poor of his *quartier* every Saturday. After Charles-Henri's death, he gave the old executioner's widow shelter in his house, and in 1819 he added the impoverished widow of his uncle Louis-Charles-Martin and her unmarried daughter to his household, knowing they had nowhere else to go. Like all of his ancestors he practiced medicine, using the formulae of his forbears, the two Charleses and Jean-Baptiste, for his lotions and unguents, dispensing the same empirical remedies to rich and poor, serving the poor free of charge.

Charles-Henri had been the first of the Sansons to receive more than the rudiments of learning. Henri received not only a very good education but developed tastes and interests that remained with him throughout his life and were passed on to his children. Very fond of music, he played the piano quite well, and was often seen at the Opéra and at the Vaudeville theater both during the Revolution and afterward. He loved to read and had a sizable library in his house. He spoke fluent English, and while serving with the National Guard, held several conversations with Thomas Paine, who in 1792 had been elected a deputy to the Convention from the département of Pas de Calais.

Like his father he enjoyed the country and derived pleasure and relaxation from the family gardens at Brie-Comte-Robert. But the fields and hillsides beyond Paris meant something more than fresh air and greenery to Henri Sanson and his wife. Marie-Louise Damidot did not cherish the idea of her children growing up in the shadow of their father's dread occupation. In Paris she knew they would be the victims of neighborhood prejudice, whereas in the country there might be a chance of protecting their innocence, at least for a few years. Young Henri-Clément spent a good part of his infancy with his grandparents at Brie-Comte-Robert, but after Charles-Henri's death, when his widow expressed sorrow at the thought of living there in the presence of so many memories, Henri decided that the time had come to sell it. There were several reasons for this decision: first of all, although the house was isolated, both the Sanson name and occupation were known in the community. Secondly, there was no school near enough so that Henri-Clément could attend classes regularly. Henri found what he wanted at Brunoy, about fifteen miles from Paris at the edge of the Forêt de Sénart. And he bought the property under the name of Longval! Once again, the Sanson family would try to escape its terrible heritage.

Henri's ambition for his son, coupled with Marie-Louise's anxiety about the boy, resulted in their leaving him at Brunoy in the care of his grandmother and a servant. He attended the local school under the name of

[178]

Longval and saw his parents only on Sundays. On the occasion of his first communion he was taken to Paris, primarily so that he could be confirmed in the church of Saint-Laurent, following family tradition, but secondly and perhaps more importantly, because his parents feared that someone in Brunoy might recognize Henri as the *bourreau,* thereby ruining their attempts to keep their son's identity secret. Having prepared for this ceremony with his schoolmates, young Henri-Clément protested that he was eager to be with his friends on this important day. But he received no explanation, no reason why they were taking him away; he was just told to accompany his parents. The boy must have been increasingly puzzled when he arrived at Saint-Laurent and learned that he would not join the other boys and girls, but would go through the ceremony alone in a small side chapel at eight o'clock in the morning.

Not until he was almost fourteen did he leave Brunoy. In 1813 his father arranged for him to attend classes at l'Institution Michel in the rue du faubourg Saint-Denis, where he was again enrolled under the name of Longval. Henri wisely decided to reveal his true identity to the principal of the establishment—asking him, however, to keep the information to himself. Henri-Clément spent from seven in the morning until six in the evening at his studies, usually returning home in the company of a schoolmate.

One evening as he reached the family dwelling, he invited his companion to come inside and meet his parents. Instead of the warm welcome he expected, he was astonished to see his father frown and act so coldly toward his guest that the youth departed in haste. At school the next day, Henri-Clément was shunned, not only by his friend of the night before, but by all the boys. This treatment continued for several days until finally, in desperation, he cornered one of them and demanded to know the reason behind the cold silence. It is not difficult to hear the sneering, derisive voice that answered, "Because your father is the executioner." Nor is it hard to feel the cruel impact of these words upon the unsuspecting Henri-Clément. Several minutes must have elapsed before a horrified and stunned fourteen-year-old realized that this answer explained a great many puzzles: why he'd lived apart from his parents, why they had insisted upon his receiving his first communion alone in Paris, why he was called Longval and not Sanson like the rest of the family. He left the Institution Michel, never to return. From that day forward, his real education began, and he discovered the meaning of his grandfather's words: an executioner can no more abdicate than a king.

Although he would not receive his formal commission until 1806 after the death of Charles-Henri, in 1795 Henri Sanson was Monsieur de Paris in fact if not in title. However, his daily work under the Directory and the Consulate was not overly burdensome. Those convicted of political crimes were no longer guillotined but shot, which meant that the executioner's job consisted of guillotining the riff-raff—thieves, murderers, rapists, common criminals. As the social standing of his victims sank to a very low level, so did his own standing in the community. What little prestige had been given the *bourreau* during the Revolution had vanished with the Terror. But in 1796, Charles-Henri would return from Brie-Comte-Robert to join his son on the scaffold for an execution that would be remembered both by the public and the Sansons alike for some time to come.

A gang of cutthroats had been terrorizing the countryside, concentrating their activities in the area of La Beauce—a flat, limestone plateau between Chartres and the forest of Orléans, known because of its wheat fields as the *grenier* (granary) *de France*. These men called themselves *Les Chauffeurs* (The Warmers), the name deriving from their habit of lighting a fire and toasting the feet of recalcitrant victims until they revealed the hiding place of jewels, money, or other valuables. Their most recent escapade had been to waylay and rob the Lyon mail coach, leaving the courier and his helper dead by the roadside. The only clues were an abandoned horse and carriage.

After an intensive search, the police found both money and mail in Château-Thierry in the possession of a man named Courriol. He and two men with him when the police arrived were arrested and taken to Paris. Nothing could be proved against the two, Golier and Guesno, and after lengthy questioning they were released. Guesno's papers had been taken from him at the time of his arrest, so he was on his way to the Préfecture de Police to secure the return of his passport when he happened to meet a friend called Lesurques, whom he persuaded to accompany him. Inside the Préfecture they were spotted by two women who promptly identified them as two of the gang. Guesno and the unfortunate Lesurques were arrested and, along with Courriol, brought before the Paris tribunal.

Courriol's mistress, Madeleine Brebant, testified to her

[181]

lover's guilt, but stated over and over again that both Guesno and Lesurques were innocent. (It was later proved that they resembled the real murderers, Vidal and Dubosc.)

Courriol himself tried to exonerate them, without success. They were condemned to death. Upon hearing of his condemnation, Lesurques said: "The crime imputed to me is atrocious and deserves death; but if it is horrible to murder on the high road, it is not less so to abuse the law and convict an innocent man. Some day my innocence will be recognized, and then my blood will fall on the jurors . . . and the judges."

On the 9th of Brumaire, year V (October 30, 1796), Charles-Henri and his son went to the Conciergerie. Lesurques, who was calm and seemingly resigned, handed Charles-Henri a sealed letter, saying: "Citizen, I hope for the honor of human justice that your functions do not often compel you to shed the blood of an innocent man; I hope that you will grant the last request of a man about to suffer for what he has not done." The letter, which Charles-Henri was permitted to open and read, was addressed to Citizen Dubosc. "I do not even know you," the condemned Lesurques had written, "and I am going to suffer the death which was reserved for you. Be satisfied with the sacrifice of my life. Should you ever be brought to account, remember my three children and their mother who are disgraced forever, and do not prolong their agony. Confess that you are the man." (Dubosc was captured and guillotined in February of 1801.)

Every few feet, as the executioner's tumbrel made its slow progress from the Conciergerie to the place de Grève, Courriol sprang to his feet and waved his arms in the air, crying: "I am guilty, Lesurques is innocent." At the foot of the scaffold he reiterated the words, pleading with executioner and spectators to help an innocent victim.

Charles-Henri, whose ears had listened to many similar protestations during his long career, recognized the ring of truth when he heard it.

"The man is innocent," he told his son. "We have executed an innocent man."

Several years thereafter, the experience would be repeated. In 1803 a complaint was lodged concerning the location of the guillotine. Nicolas Frochot, préfect of the département of the Seine, whose office in the Hôtel de Ville overlooked the place de Grève, objected to the tumult caused by the immense crowds that congregated beneath his windows on the days of execution, and to the guillotine which was the reason for their presence. He asked that the instrument be moved to the place Maubert in the Latin quarter, which had been the site of public executions and whippings during the sixteenth century.

The authorities did not concur, and a heated dispute finally resulted in a compromise; executions would take place not at the place Maubert, but down by the Seine. The guillotine's first victim in this new location was a grocer named Trumeau, condemned for having poisoned his daughter and his niece with arsenic. Once again, Charles-Henri (in Paris to assist his son) knew that his victim was not guilty as charged. Having neither his father's experience nor his perspicacity, Henri apparently held no such thought. Not until long afterward, when quite by accident he opened his father's register, did he discover a marginal note. Beside the name of Trumeau, the old executioner had written the words: "Again a Lesurques."

[183]

The years of the Directory and the Consulate, although not busy ones for Henri Sanson, were important years for France. Politically, socially, and militarily she was on the ascendancy in Europe. Prussia, Holland, and Spain had made peace in 1795, and Napoleon's Italian campaign had brought Sardinia, Milan, and Genoa into French possession; Belgium was annexed to France. In 1797 Austria was forced to sign the treaty of Campo Formio, leaving only Great Britain at war. Bonaparte, deeming a direct attact on Britain to be too hazardous, decided to strike at the English by invading Egypt; from there, he planned to attack the British posts in India. The battle of the Nile in August of 1798 resulted in the destruction of the French fleet, temporarily delaying Napoleon's dreams of glory. To buttress its victory, Britain drew Austria and Russia into a new alliance for the purpose of confronting the French army in Italy. Although French forces were checked by an Austro-Russian army, Bonaparte managed to slip through the British blockade and return to France in October of 1799. In December of that year, the French people approved the constitution of the year VIII, granting him dictatorial powers for ten years.

The Directory soon became a Consulate with the little Corsican as First Consul. A second Italian campaign in 1800 ended with the victory at Marengo, and in December of that year the Austrian army was routed. Russia withdrew from the coalition in 1801, and in 1802 the treaty of Amiens established France as the principal power in Europe. That year (the year X) a constitutional amendment awarded Bonaparte with the office of Consul for life. In 1804 he was crowned Emperor, thus beginning a decade of triumph that would not end until June 18, 1815, at the Battle of Waterloo.

Of the many reforms instituted by Napoleon—his religious concordat, his centralized form of government, his state schools, his rebuilding of roads and bridges, his tax reform—the Code Napoleon would be the most important, not only for France but also because it would form the basis for civil law in most of the countries of Europe. It assured Frenchmen of equality before the law regardless of rank, wealth, or religion. For the Sanson family, in fact for the entire confrèrie of executioners, it was the beginning of the end.

But if Henri Sanson's schedule was not as crowded as his father's had been, at the end of his career he had nonetheless participated in over three hundred and sixty executions. Following the death of Lesurques, he traveled to Vendôme in May of 1797 to assist his uncle Nicolas-Charles-Gabriel Sanson (then executioner of Blois) and the executioner of Chartres in decapitating Babeuf and Darthé, condemned for having plotted against the Directory. In March of 1798, he and the executioners of Versailles and Auxerre assisted Nicolas Jouënne, executioner of Melun, in decapitating six *Chauffeurs* who had been terrorizing the population of the Seine-et-Marne district. In 1803 he beheaded Trumeau, the grocer, and in 1804 Georges Cadoudal and eleven accomplices went to the guillotine for having conspired to kill Napoleon.

On May 16, 1808, Henri and his aides went to the Conciergerie to escort to the guillotine a murderer who had languished in jail for two years while controversy raged in the salons and shops of Paris over whether justice had been served. La fille Bonhourt, known as Manette, had committed not one murder but many. A pretty, vivacious blonde, she had fallen in love with a man. Believing his attestations of love and his promise to marry her, she had let him seduce her. Her carefree lover

[185]

not only had deserted her but had jeered at her desperate attempts to ensnare him. Realizing at last that her efforts were in vain, she swore revenge—on all men. For the purpose, she dressed in men's clothing. This beautiful young girl's blonde hair fell from beneath a man's top hat, her tight-fitting coat enhanced the shapeliness of her body, and her white culottes and black leather boots revealed long slim legs. The startling and intriguing effect fascinated and attracted a masculine population whose jaded palates were ever in search of the unusual.

Manette would lure her victim to a hotel room, where she persuaded him to order wine. She then managed, at some point during the evening, to divert the man's attention long enough to drop an opiate into his glass. While he slept, she pulled a hammer from her reticule and bludgeoned him to death. Instead of departing immediately, she spent the night in the hotel room. The following morning, having robbed the corpse of whatever money and jewels she could find, she instructed the hotel clerk to leave her "husband" alone. "He is sleeping late and does not wish to be disturbed," she would say. "I am going shopping and shall return at noon." Invariably the clerk was so astonished by her costume that when questioned by the police, he could only shake his head and offer the vague statement that the woman had been pretty and blonde. And, inasmuch as she always changed back into feminine attire, she became no more noticeable than any other pretty Parisienne. Despite the intensive search that agents of Fouché, the Minister of Police, conducted after every one of these murders, Manette eluded capture for a number of years.

A police agent finally trapped her. Having let himself be lured into a hotel room, he drank her potion, but managed to call for help before sleep overcame him.

Hotel employees came running into the room in time to stop Manette, whose hammer was poised to strike. Arrested and taken to prison, she confessed, boasting that she had killed eighteen or twenty men—she couldn't remember the exact number. She also confessed to having murdered a girl named Marge or Manje, whom she suspected of recognizing her. Amazingly enough—probably because of her beauty—the case inspired sympathy; so much so that pleas for clemency reached the desk of the Emperor himself. Her appeal was denied, but instead of rendering its decision in a matter of weeks, as was customary, the appeals court let the verdict dangle for two years.

Even the hard-hearted custodians at the Conciergerie succumbed to her charm, expressing admiration and pity for the smiling prisoner who lost none of her loveliness during her confinement. On the day of execution, she changed her skirts for masculine attire, saying that she would go to her death in her costume of revenge. She submitted without complaint to the cutting of her blonde curls, offered no resistance when her wrists were strapped together behind her back. Henri and his aides transported her to the place de Grève, where an immense crowd awaited them, eyeing Sanson's tumbrel with avid curiosity and with no small amount of admiration for this calm, smiling woman, who maintained her composure to the last.

"Don't you think it a pity," she said to Henri as he led her to the guillotine, "to cut off a head as beautiful as mine?"

The executioner was finding his task more and more distasteful and loathsome. He tried to ease his conscience by the practice of medicine, by his donations of bread to the poor, by living as quiet and as dignified a life (outside of his work) as possible, and by repeating over and over again: "I am only the instrument, it is justice that strikes." To one who questioned him about his feelings after he had guillotined a man, he replied, "I feel no more remorse than anyone who is required to be present at an execution." He spoke the words, but could not believe them. Try as he might, he never succeeded in convincing himself of their truth. The only reason he continued was the knowledge that without this job, he would be penniless.

There were dozens of executioners—not to mention their sons, wives, widows, and other relatives—whose work and means of earning a livelihood ended with the Revolution. Only a handful managed to procure small pensions from the government; the remainder found themselves in dire poverty. A vivid example of what happened when executioners tried to earn a living by other means was an occurrence within the Sanson family. Louis-Gabriel Sanson, son of Louis-Cyr-Charlemagne (executioner of Provins and cousin to Henri), decided to abandon the family profession and strike out on his own. Leaving his parents' home, he settled in Troyes, where he apprenticed himself to an ironsmith. Encouraged that no one had seemed to recognize his name during his apprenticeship, he opened a locksmith's shop, only to discover that no one remains anonymous in a provincial town; local curiosity cannot tolerate it. The moment word circulated regarding Louis-Gabriel's ancestry, no one came near him. He had no choice but to close his shop and move back to Provins. Completely dependent upon his mother, Marie-Marguerite Gendron, who by then was a widow living on a pension of four hundred francs a year, he returned to the *maison du bourreau* situated outside the walls of Provins—a small stone dwelling that is still standing today. When his mother's pension ceased at her death, he became dependent upon the municipality of Provins for his meager and miserable existence.

Other members of the Sanson family felt poverty reach out for them, as witness the following letters preserved in the Archives. The first is addressed to Monsieur Dupont, Minister of Justice and Keeper of the Seals:

> Nicolas-Gabriel-Charles Sanson, executioner of Reims has the honor of presenting to you the picture of his unhappy situation. Brother to the late executioner of Paris, he served with him for eighteen years. . . . Monsieur, he throws himself at your feet, pleading with you to ask the Minister of the Interior to accord the petitioner the help that is vital to his subsistence and to his infirmities by granting him a pension in whatever amount you choose; the suppliant will never cease to pray God to bless your precious life.

The document is signed by Nicolas Sanson.

This letter having been unsuccessful, a second missive was addressed to Messieurs composant Le Comité De Legislation.

> Nicolas-Gabriel-Charles Sanson, executioner of Criminal Judgments of the city of Reims, aged seventy-one years, has the honor of presenting to you his unhappy situation; he has served in this capacity for thirty years with never the slightest reprimand from magistrates. . . . Because of personal misfortune and the suppression of his salary and revenues, he was obliged to leave the aforementioned city and seek refuge with his nephew, the executioner of Paris, who was kind enough to receive him, and to give him shelter and food. . . . I dare to hope that you will not refuse my plea.

This bore the signature, "Sanson, c/o his nephew, Rue Saint-Jean."

A letter to the Minister of Justice from Louis-Charles-Martin Sanson, executioner of Tours, pleads for reemployment: Louis-Victor Sanson, aged twenty-two, "Son of Citizen Sanson, formerly executioner of Tours, département of Indre-et-Loire, assistant to his uncle, the executioner of Blois and cousin of Sanson who is executioner of Paris, has the honor of asking for employment. . . ."

The Sansons were not alone in their plight; a pathetic letter from Limoges expresses the desperate situation of a provincial *bourreau:*

> Jean Simaillaud, father of a large family, throws himself upon your mercy. . . . Having been

assistant to the executioner of Limoges . . . he
pleads with your excellency to find him a job as
executioner. In spite of having received a notice
stating that his request, numbered 8020 had been
placed under consideration by your office, he is
still among the forgotten. . . .

The number referred to by the man from Limoges
appeared on a printed form sent out by the Ministry of
Justice which, if 8020 is any indication, must have been
flooded with requests. This piece of paper displayed a
letterhead with the words, *République Française; Liberté,
Égalité, Fraternité,* and the picture of Justice holding her
scales. The printed message stated that the citizen's
letter, written on such and such a day (date to be filled
in), had been received, and that his petition (nature of
request to be filled in) would be taken under consideration. Beneath were the words: *Salut et Fraternité* and a
space for the scrawled (and no doubt illegible) signature
of some minor official.

Many executioners were uprooted, transferred to new
posts; and this, too, caused hardship and suffering.
"Settled for many years at Issoudun," writes executioner
Desfourneaux, "where he has a house and a family, the
sole support of his mother and several sisters, neither he
nor his relatives wish to leave a locality where the years
have softened people's opinion of us. . . . The difficulty
of finding a place to live and the exorbitant prices
demanded because of prejudice against us makes this
move even more distressing." The executioner on Corsica
was equally miserable. "Citizen Minister, you must know
that I have a wife and a large family. The high cost of
living on Corsica makes it almost impossible for me to
feed my family. I am most unhappy here. . . ."

Most of these pathetic requests and pleas were probably buried in the files or thrown out with the trash.

Someone in officialdom must have had a conscience or a kind heart, however, because charts exist listing the executioners' widows, giving name, age, place of domicile, means of support if any, and the amount of money (a pittance) proposed by the government for their welfare.

As executioner of Paris, Henri Sanson was in a happier situation than his confrères. Because there were fewer executions to perform, he had been able to reduce the number of his aides to two, no longer requiring the seven or nine that his father had needed during the Revolution. And his salary remained the same. A further advantage existed in that the government now reimbursed him for his expenses; and inasmuch as no one seemed to check them, he indulged in a bit of exaggeration. These sources of income, plus the money he earned in the practice of medicine, made his living a comfortable one.

However, he was quite aware that not only were executions on the decrease, but that a new, and to him alarming, trend of thought menaced his livelihood. "Every day," he is quoted as having said to an acquaintance, "the efforts of philanthropists threaten my existence, as they continue to speak out for the suppression of capital punishment. I assure you, Monsieur, that it would be a great pity if this occurred, because not one of the persons who has passed our way could have been rehabilitated, had he been given his life"—a harsh statement from a man who loathed his job and pitied his victims, perhaps delivered in the hope that it would be quoted in the public press and stem the tide of public opinion, preserving his job and protecting his income. As Monsieur de Paris, Henri would be the last to suffer the loss of his position, but how long would that position exist? Under the Bourbon *Restoration* (1814–1830), his salary would be slashed to twelve thousand francs a year, and under Louis-Philippe to a mere eight thousand.

But Henri Sanson knew that fears, doubts, and worries must be put aside. The die had been cast almost two centuries earlier, and his future had been arranged for him before he was born. The future would be no different for Henri-Clément, and the sooner the boy realized it, the easier life would be for him. But Henri-Clément had no desire to proceed in his father's footsteps; "I shall never have the courage to guillotine a man," he said to his grandmother, Marie-Anne Jugier, who had been his confidante at Brie-Comte-Robert and at Brunoy, and who was now living with her son in Paris. "You have no choice" was the reply given him by the old woman, and by Henri. "The sooner you get used to the place de Grève, the better."

Terrified of what was to come, sixteen-year-old Henri-Clément steeled himself for his first experience on the scaffold. The execution scheduled to take place on March 20, 1815, was that of an army officer, a lieutenant named Dautun, dismissed by the Bourbon monarchy and subsequently sentenced to the guillotine for the murder of his brother and his aunt. But something far more significant, far more important to the French people than the execution of an ex-army officer, would mark the calendar on March 20, 1815.

In 1812, Napoleon Bonaparte—whose victorious *Grande Armée* had subjugated most of Europe—had decided to move half a million men to the Russian frontier. After defeating the Russians at Borodino in September, he marched on Moscow, only to be forced into an ignominious and disastrous retreat five weeks later. From that point on, his mighty empire began to collapse. Finally in April of 1814, he was forced to abdicate. Granted a pension of two million francs a year and sovereignty over the island of Elba, he departed. Louis XVIII, brother of Louis XVI, was proclaimed king of France. But, in February of 1815, Napoleon escaped from his island kingdom and on March 1st he landed at Cannes on the southern coast of France. Having followed the ex-emperor's progress northward—Grenoble on March 7th, Lyon on the 10th, Fontainbleau on the 19th—the people eagerly awaited his arrival at the Tuileries Palace on March 20th.

Louis XVIII had been a colorless figure compared to the fiery little Corsican. Not only did the French see in Bonaparte the hope of a proud future for their nation, but both the peasants and the bourgeoisie feared and mistrusted the restoration government, suspicious that the word "restoration" might mean a restoration of privilege and rank. A rousing welcome awaited the exile. And, aware that enthusiastic crowds would jam every street, the Ministry of Justice decided that it could not permit anything as sordid as an execution to mar the Emperor's triumphant entry into his capital city. The execution was postponed until March 29th.

Henri-Clément breathed a sigh of relief. He even dared to hope that Napoleon, a military man himself, might pardon an ex-officer. But no act of clemency was forthcoming. Even if the news of an execution had reached the Emperor's desk, it is more than probable that the task of organizing an army would take precedence over the fate of one misguided and unfortunate soldier.

On March 29th, Henri and his son escorted their victim to the place de Grève as scheduled, the poor man screaming his innocence the entire length of the route. Sickened by the sound of Dautun's repeated cry of "I am innocent, I am innocent," Henri-Clément averted his eyes when the guillotine's blade descended, then fled from the scene with tears streaming unashamedly down his cheeks.

He acquitted himself no more honorably on the occasion of his first trip to the scaffold as executioner. In 1819 Henri succumbed to an attack of pleurisy and was unable to rise from his bed. On January 13th Henri-Clément and his assistants went to fetch their prisoner, a member of the Light Infantry of the *Garde Royale* named Foulard, who had been convicted of murder. (He had killed two women for the sole purpose of stealing a watch and some gold earrings.) The executioner describes the scene himself: "We arrived at the place de Grève. The guillotine stretched its two huge red arms into the sky, and the pale rays of a winter sun danced on the polished steel of its blade." The Abbé Montès, a priest known for his aid to the condemned, turned to Henri-Clément and asked him if he had taken his father's place. When the executioner nodded, he said: "It takes courage to carry out your task. We walk toward the same end, you and I, but by different roads. You represent the justice of man, and I the mercy of God. May I ask a favor in His name? Please do not give the signal to begin until this poor child pronounces the words: 'God, I commit my soul to your keeping.'"

The "poor child" was twenty years old—the same age as his executioner!

Henri-Clément could not even mount the steps to the scaffold. Knowing that there was no escape, that he must legalize the proceedings by his presence, but realizing that he could not summon the strength to perform the task himself, he ordered his first assistant Fauconnier to assume command. And then, while subordinates carried out his duties, Henri-Clément Sanson, the seventh generation of his family to hold the title of Monsieur de Paris, stood at the foot of the wooden stairway like a frightened child. Witnesses reported that when the moment came, he flinched as if the heavy blade had come down upon his own neck.

Henri's illness was of considerable duration and it forced his son to become familiar with the journey from prison to scaffold. But Henri-Clément never conquered his revulsion for the guillotine, never managed to complete his task without visible signs of loathing and disgust. His grandfather's admonition, "we must live where fate has placed us," drummed into his ears by every member of his family, undoubtedly played an important part in his decision to remain in the profession of his forebears. But the necessity of earning enough money to support a wife forced his surrender. In 1817, mere months after the execution of Foulard, Henri-Clément Sanson celebrated his marriage to Virginie-Emilie Lefébure in the church of Saint-Laurent. The girl, daughter of Jean-Baptiste Alexis Lefébure, purveyor of woolens and hosiery in the faubourg Saint-Denis, had not been brought up within the confrèrie of executioners, but neither was she a complete outsider, as her parents had been friendly with the Sansons for some years.

The marriage was not a happy one. Henri-Clément had submitted to his fate, but he never accepted it. The couple lived at 31 bis rue du Marais with Henri, his wife, and a group of impoverished Sansons from the provinces, who had been taken in by their Paris relative when they had nowhere else to go. Added to this collection of executioners, their wives, and offspring, were Henri's aides. To further emphasize the family profession, one room in the house had been set aside to exhibit Henri's collection of ancient instruments of torture. Escape from all phases of the detested milieu had been rendered impossible. Despite changes made by Henri-Clément after his father's death in 1840, such as replacing the iron grillwork with an elegant doorway and building a glassed-in veranda, the house would always be the *maison du bourreau,* and its master, try as he might, could not delude himself into believing it would ever be anything else.

Henri returned to the scaffold, greatly weakened by his attack of pleurisy. From that time on, his son would assist him, and with increasing frequency and ever-growing revulsion, replace him.

Henri-Clément, the last Sanson to hold the title of executioner, would guillotine 111 people during his lifetime, his list of victims a mere fraction of his grandfather's roster. But his life, far more than that of Charles-Henri, would prove the truth of that little verse in the eighteenth-century *Almanach des Prisons:* having made all else perish, what is left for the executioner except to destroy himself?

A gambler, a spendthrift, and ultimately a sexual pervert, Henri-Clément would do just that.

The Revolution had destroyed the feudal laws, the outmoded institutions, and the privileges enjoyed by the Church and the nobility. Napoleon reorganized the nation, gave it a stable monetary system, a religious concordat, a code of laws. He centralized the government, set up an educational system, and initiated a fair method of taxation. But both the Revolution and the Empire had been periods of turbulence, of slaughter at home and abroad, and neither anarchy nor dictatorship had proved a satisfactory answer to France's political unrest. The people were now willing to try a return to monarchy, but a limited monarchy, one that would not abrogate the hard-won principles of *Liberté, Égalité, Fraternité*. Louis XVIII, eager to compromise his beliefs in the interests of peace and justice, granted his subjects a charter that preserved the best of the Napoleonic legacy, and in addition promised them a bicameral legislature with a Chamber of Peers and a Chamber of Deputies. Left to his own devices, he might have succeeded in attaining the peace and calm he so desperately desired. But the return of the Bourbon monarchy made possible the return of the *emigrés*, the thousands of embittered aristocrats who had fled France and suffered the hardship and the privation of exile. They could not, and would not, forget what had happened to them in 1789 and 1793. They detested the new society, and the ruler whom they labeled a "Jacobin King" because he had compromised the tenets of absolutism. They were determined to bring back the *ancien régime*. Led by the King's brother, the comte d'Artois (the future Charles X), their goal was reprisal, vengeance. By packing the legislature, they managed to drive Louis XVIII toward a policy of reaction which was to result in the Revolution of 1830.

A movement known as *La Terreur Blanche* (The White Terror) sprang into being and spread through France like a virus, its goal the punishment of all revolutionaries, all who had voted for the death of Louis XVI, all

Bonapartists, everyone who had fought in Napoleon's *Grande Armée.* And if the White Terror sought the death of all who had in any way harmed the persons of Louis XVI and Marie Antoinette, surely the executioner and his family should have headed the list of wanted criminals.

But once again the Sansons were untouched, their position seemingly unassailable. Just as in 1789, when as servants of the King they should have been as vulnerable as any other royal official, the revolutionaries had not only left them unharmed but used them to enforce the new laws, so now the royalists ignored them, assuming that they would continue to execute the condemned in accordance with the orders handed to them by the courts of justice.

This failure to identify the executioner with a government, with public opinion, with human emotions, was in effect a failure to admit his existence as a person. Had he been a clerk in a government office, the fact that his job continued despite a change in regime would not have been surprising. But he held a commission which should have meant his dismissal in 1789, just as it ought to have done under the Bourbon Restoration. Apart from the fact that executioners, being a special breed of men, were difficult to replace, a possible explanation is that they were, in all probability, deemed unworthy of concern: they themselves could find no other work, and for that reason would be loyal and faithful to whatever form of government paid them. And, being credited with neither intelligence nor feelings nor standing in the community, the executioner posed no threat to monarchy or republic, for he belonged to nothing—and to no one. He was a machine, an instrument of justice. He and the guillotine were one.

[199]

A plot to kill Louis XVIII provided Henri Sanson and his son with three victims. Article 13 of the penal code, an atavistic statute, stated that: "A man condemned to death for parricide shall be led to the place of execution in his shirt sleeves, barefooted, his head covered by a black veil. He shall stand on the scaffold while the bailiff reads his sentence aloud to the public; he shall then have his right hand amputated, and immediately thereafter, be executed." (Amputation would be suppressed in 1832.) The three men found guilty of the plot were named Tolleron, Carbonneau, and Pleignier; and as large a crowd gathered to witness their torture and execution as had ever congregated during the Terror; the cries of "Vive le Roi" were as vociferous and as bloodthirsty now as had been the demands for the head of Louis XVI in 1793. Henri-Clément, whose agony rivaled that of the culprits, did not even try to mount the steps to the scaffold.

Charles-Ferdinand, duc de Berry, was the younger son of the future Charles X. On June 7, 1820, Louis-Pierre Louvel, a saddler by trade, went to the guillotine for having murdered him as he was coming out of the Opéra. A fanatical republican, Louvel confessed that his aim in life had been to extinguish every member of the Bourbon line. Men, women, and children lined the streets to see him pass, among them a young Victor Hugo, who reported on the occasion many years later in his *Choses vues*:

> I remember, [he wrote,] that in my extreme
> youth, I saw Louvel crossing the Pont-au-Change
> on the day when they took him to the place de
> Grève. It was, if I remember correctly, in the
> month of June. The sun shone brightly. Louvel

was in a tumbrel, his arms tied behind his back, a
blue redingote thrown over his shoulders, a round
hat on his head. He was pale. I saw only his
profile. Every part of him seemed to breathe a
kind of grave, somber ferocity, a violent strength
of purpose. . . .

In September of 1822, four young fanatics known as
the Conspirators of La Rochelle met their death on the
scaffold, convicted of having plotted the downfall of the
Bourbons. But unlike Louvel, they had killed no one. All
four refused the ministrations of the Abbé Montès and all
four died courageously. The last one to be guillotined
stepped forward, as had Louis XVI, to address the
spectators. "My brothers," he shouted, "if I cry, it is not
for my own fate, but for that of my poor comrades, all of
whom have perished in front of my eyes. In shedding our
blood for you, we leave you a gift of vengeance.
Remember our last wish, Long live Liberty!"

Henri-Clément was not the only man affected by this
display of bravery. Soldiers fell to their knees, and some
of the spectators fainted. The public was neither as
stony-hearted nor as unfeeling as it had imagined itself to
be.

Not all punishments were as dramatic as those meted
out to political prisoners. Pierre Coignard, an escaped
convict who had followed a life of crime, was branded
and sentenced to stand in the pillory. General Sarrazin,
convicted of polygamy, was reputed to have wives in
France, England, and Italy. He was delivered to the
Sansons, whose orders specified the *carcan*, or public
exhibition in the pillory with an iron collar about the
neck, prior to imprisonment. The Abbé Contrafatto,
alleged to have violated a five-year-old girl (and later

proved innocent of the crime) found himself condemned to an hour in the pillory and a prison sentence. Among those convicted of murder was Pierre-Louis Martin, who was led to the scaffold with a black veil over his head, and in accordance with the law against parricides (he had killed his father) his fist was cut off before decapitation. Six months thereafter, Nicolas Boutillier received the same sentence for having murdered his mother.

The number of executions diminished radically. Sometimes months elapsed without any need for the services of the Sansons *père et fils*. As executions and even punishments declined, so did the need for the services of executioners. The Sansons occupying the post in Paris were the ranking members of the confrèrie; as executioners in smaller towns in the vicinity were relieved of their duties, Henri and Henri-Clément performed whatever services might be required in Versailles, in Beauvais, in Compiègne. In less than a decade, a royal ordinance would eliminate the jobs of many more of their relatives and friends.

The reigns of Louis XVIII and Charles X saw a rebirth of absolutism and a return of the privileges of the nobility. Charles X, far more stubborn and despotic than his predecessor, chose to ignore the signs and portents, the rebellious anger of the Chamber of Deputies. Defying the desires of his subjects, he appointed the Prince de Polignac as Prime Minister. He sought to limit the freedom of the press and dissolved the recalcitrant Chamber, but failed in his attempt to pack the new one with his friends. Finally, acknowledging defeat, he fled to England. A bourgeois majority succeeded in overcoming the opposition of Legitimists and Bonapartists and gave the throne to fifty-six-year-old Louis-Philippe, duc d'Orléans (son of Philippe Égalité)—a simple, down-to-earth family man, a "citizen king" who looked and acted more like a shopkeeper than a sovereign. His famous pear-shaped head, no less than the umbrella he always carried, would make him the target of every cartoonist and satirist in the realm.

This colorless monarch's reign from 1830 to 1848 would see the beginning of a strong, nationwide movement of vital importance to the Sansons—a concerted effort by sociologists, writers, painters, and men of politics to abolish capital punishment.

In 1829 a short piece of fiction appeared in the Paris bookshops. Supposedly found in a prison cell, it was presented as the scribbling of a man under sentence of death, written during his last hours before going to the scaffold. The work was anonymous, but rumor placed it as a translation, its author an Englishman or an American. In 1832 it was published again, this time with a preface and the name of its author displayed on the title page: *Le Dernier Jour d'un condamné,* by Victor Hugo.

Twenty-seven years old when the novelette appeared, Hugo had already witnessed more than one execution. "The author did not get the idea for this piece in a book, he is not in the habit of searching for his ideas in such remote places," wrote Hugo in the preface. "He saw it where everyone can see such things, quite plainly and simply on the place de Grève. There, when passing by one day, he picked up this fatal idea, which was lying in a pool of blood under the bloody stumps of the guillotine."

Le Dernier Jour d'un condamné caused considerable comment, but little sympathy for the plight it described so vividly and so poignantly:

> Condemned to death!
>
> For five weeks I have lived with this thought, ever alone with it, ever chilled by its presence, ever crushed by its weight.
>
> I have just made my will.
>
> Why? I am condemned to pay costs, and everything I have will barely cover them. The guillotine is terribly expensive.
>
> I leave a mother, I leave a wife, I leave a child.
>
> A little girl three years old, gentle, rosy, fragile, with huge black eyes and long chestnut hair.
>
> She was two years and one month old when I saw her for the last time.
>
> Thus, after my death, three women; without a son, without a husband, without a father; three orphans, three widows because of the law.
>
> I admit that I should be justly punished; but these innocent victims, what have they done? What difference does it make? They have been disgraced, ruined. That is justice.

And later, describing the prison, Hugo writes:

> People were standing near the door and along the walls; besides the priest and the gendarmes, there were also three men.

The first, the tallest, the oldest, was fat and had a red face. He wore a redingote and a shapeless tricorn. It was he! It was the *bourreau,* the servant of the guillotine. The two others were his assistants.

Hugo released the full force of his scorn for the executioner in the preface, published in 1832. In recalling the debates which took place in Parlement during October of 1830 on the subject of capital punishment, he says:

The *bourreau,* if truth must be told, was a very frightened man. On the day when he heard our lawmakers speak of humanity, philanthropy, progress, he thought himself lost. He hid himself, the wretched creature, he cowered beneath his guillotine, as uncomfortable in the July sun as a nocturnal bird in daylight. No one saw him for six months. He showed no signs of life. Little by little, however, he regained confidence, as he lurked in the darkness. He cocked an ear in the direction of the Chamber and heard no mention of his name . . . they were occupied with other matters of grave social consequence, such as a subsidy for the Opéra-Comique . . . no one gave him a thought, that head-chopper. Aware of this, the man relaxed, he stuck his head out of his hole and looked around; he took a step, then two, like the mice of La Fontaine, then he dared to emerge from under his scaffold. . . .

Hugo concluded his diatribe against the death penalty: "The social structure of the past rested upon three columns; the priest, the king, the *bourreau*. Years ago a voice said 'the gods have gone!' Recently another voice was lifted and cried, 'the kings have gone!' It is now time for a third voice to cry *'le bourreau s'en va!'* "

The third voice proved but a faint cry. The Chamber of Deputies voted for the abolition of capital punishment, the Chamber of Peers to retain it. But Hugo had not capitulated. That same year (1832) the *Revue de Paris* published his *Claude Gueux*, the true story of a felon by that name. Once again, Hugo attacked society for creating criminals, and justice for its unjust and senseless cruelty. In 1845 he would begin writing a novel, which he called *Les Misères*; soon afterward he changed the title to *Jean Tréjean*. By the time he had finished the work in 1861, he had decided to call it *Les Misérables*, and as such it would gain fame as both social commentary and literary triumph.

Although far from successful in his quest, Victor Hugo's words had not fallen upon completely deaf ears. "In view of the diminution of condemnations," states a royal ordinance of 1832, "it becomes possible to reduce the number of executioners . . . and their aides. . . ." It goes on to specify the changes, both in numbers and in salary:

Article 1. The actual number of executioners shall be cut in half. There shall be no replacements.

Article 2. In future there shall be but one aide to the executioner in the départements of Calvados, Corsica, Eure. . . .

There shall be two aides in the département of the Seine Inférieure and four in the département of the Seine. . . .

Article 3. Executioners' wages:

[206]

Executioner residing in Paris	8,000 francs
Executioner of Lyon	5,000 francs
Executioners of Bordeaux & Rouen	4,000 francs
In cities with a population of over 50,000 inhabitants	3,500 francs
Cities of 20,000 to 50,000	2,400 francs
Cities of 20,000 and under	2,000 francs

This law eliminated every one of the Sanson family from the roster of executioners except *Monsieur de Paris.* Even Henri must have felt a cold wind upon his back, for to add to his concerns, the place of execution was moved from its central location on the place de Grève (in front of the Hôtel de Ville) to the Rond Point de la Barrière Saint-Jacques at the southern tip of Paris, to a neighborhood not only removed but unsavory. This decision answered the complaints of officials with offices in the City Hall who objected to the sight of so much blood beneath their windows; it minimized the importance of executions, and was intended to discourage large crowds from gathering to witness them.

In a period such as the 1830s, when everything seemed to indicate a growing awareness of social injustice, when for the first time the words "attenuating circumstances" appeared in the legal code, one might expect to find that the executioner would fade into oblivion. But strangely enough, quite the reverse was true. Executions diminished, but the executioner suddenly became one of the most sought-after personalities in Paris. The phenomenon, caused in some part by the writings of Victor Hugo, was actually due to the man who had initiated the request that the guillotine be moved to its now remote location.

Benjamin-Nicolas-Marie Appert (1797–1847), philan-

[207]

thropist and member of the Societé Royale des Prisons de France, had started professional life as a teacher. Learning that a great many soldiers could neither read nor write, he had obtained permission from the Ministry of War to establish schools in military regiments. Because of his efforts, over a hundred thousand men received the rudiments of an education. His next venture, a more daring and less fortunate experiment, took him into the prisons. While he was engaged in teaching a group of convicts, two of the men under his tutelage escaped. Appert, whose sympathy for his students was well known, suddenly found himself on the wrong side of the law. Thrown into La Force prison, he experienced at first hand the rigors of prison discipline and the misery of prison life. From the moment of his release until his death, he devoted his time to bettering conditions for convicts, traveling to prisons all over Europe in pursuit of information and knowledge. He published a treatise on elementary education for prisoners, edited a monthly publication, *Le Journal des prisons*, and compiled a four-volume work entitled *Bagnes, Prisons et criminels*. Respected by lawyers and magistrates no less than by ministers and high officials in the government of Louis Philippe, Benjamin Appert was also admired by many distinguished men of letters. He appears in Stendhal's *Le Rouge et le Noir* under his real name; his part in the novel is the same role he played in life:

> That fine gentleman from Paris, so obnoxious to the mayor of Verrières, was none other than M. Appert, [writes Stendhal,] who two days before, had found a way of getting into not only the prison and the workhouse of Verrières, but the hospital as well, which was directed gratis by the

[208]

mayor and the chief property owners of the vicinity.

"But," said Madame de Rênal timidly, "what harm can this gentleman from Paris do you, since you administer the poor fund with the most scrupulous honesty?"

"He has come for the sole purpose of finding fault; afterward he will write articles for the Liberal newspapers."

Benjamin Appert's reputation as a diligent and determined social worker preceded him, and he was known and feared by those in charge of provincial institutions, as well as those in the larger cities.

A man engaged in research on prisons and criminals would quite logically seek out the executioner as a primary source of information, so it is not surprising that Appert knew both Henri Sanson and his son. The Sansons, usually sensitive and suspicious of anyone who probed into their activities, were quick to realize that Benjamin Appert was neither a curiosity seeker nor a journalist whose sole desire and intent was to lampoon or denigrate them. Having questioned them more than once during his visits to the Palais de Justice, the philanthropist treated them as equals, and they were flattered by the genuine interest shown them by a man in his position.

Appert's interest in social reform was shared by one of his friends, Sir John Bowring, an official of the British government accredited to Paris. Bowring, who knew Paris well, had been asked to act as guide and companion to John George, Viscount Lambton, Count of Durham, son-in-law of Lord Grey, in whose cabinet Durham held the office of Lord Privy Seal. Durham, head of the Liberal party in England, had come to Paris

[209]

to investigate social conditions and to ascertain what had been accomplished in reform of both the educational and the penal systems. Bowring introduced Lord Durham to Benjamin Appert, and one evening, when Durham, Mr. Edward Ellice (his uncle by marriage), and Bowring were dining with Appert, the Englishmen asked their host to introduce them to the executioner. Appert, in his book *Dix ans à la Cour Du Roi Louis-Philippe*, describes the event:

Lord Durham and Lord Ellice, Minister of War for Britain, came together with my worthy friend Bowring to visit me, Quai d'Orsay, to arrange a meeting with Sanson, who had offered to set up the guillotine for these gentlemen. I went to forewarn the executioner that we would visit him on the following Saturday. As this was the first time I had entered his house [in the Rue des Marais] he expressed delight at the prospect of receiving me.

Madame Sanson opened the door, and when she learned my name, she was most cordial, and immediately summoned her husband, who hastened to remove the cotton cap that covered his high forehead and bald pate. He greeted me with an embarrassing show of respect and deference, and insisted that I sit in his armchair, a prospect I must admit that did not particularly appeal to me; again a prejudice. I noticed religious pictures all around the room, I heard someone playing *l'air de la Muette* on the piano [it was his granddaughter]. I thought of all the unfortunates that Sanson had executed, I saw with horror the double-edged blade marked with two grooves, one of which reminded me of the execution of M. de Lally, the other of the Chevalier de la Barre; I was startled when Sanson said: "Monsieur, the armchair in which you are sitting has been in our family for many years, my father and those close to him were very fond of it and always used it." I don't know why, but involuntarily I got to my feet and took my leave.

The following Saturday, Lord Durham came for me in his carriage. . . . He had mentioned our visit to the rue des Marais to so many English people that the number of carriages following ours made us look like a funeral procession. Lord Durham asked me, as we rode along, whether it might be possible to buy a sheep, so as to see the guillotine in action. I replied that such a thing might cause, and with reason, severe criticism, and he did not insist. . . . He [Sanson] was attired in formal black, and led us to the bank of the Saint-Martin canal, to the house of a painter who was the custodian of the fatal instrument. There, the British character showed itself for what it is, each man wanted to touch the blade, the baskets, to lie down on the *bascule.*

Sir John Bowring, in his *Autobiographical Recollections*, adds that Henry Sanson referred to his guillotine as *La Méchanique*, that the frightful instrument was painted red, and that for this demonstration, a man had been constructed out of straw. (The curiosity of the English ladies and gentlemen—there were ladies present at this lurid event—had undoubtedly been piqued by an exhibit in Madame Tussaud's London waxworks. The former Marie Grosholtz had recreated the death of Louis XVI, with the king lying on the *bascule*, his head in the *lunette*, and Charles-Henri Sanson and his aides in attendance. A

[211]

printed sign explained that the blade of the reconstructed guillotine was the "real" one.)

Helping the Sansons in their demonstration was a man named François-Eugène Vidocq, a character so incredible, so fascinating, so intriguing to the Paris of Louis-Philippe that he was immortalized in the works of three literary giants of the period—Victor Hugo, Honoré de Balzac, and Alexandre Dumas.

Vidocq, the son of a baker in Arras, had run away from home at an early age and joined the army, serving under General Dumouriez. Jailed for forgery, he was sentenced to eight years at hard labor and sent to the galleys at Brest. Twice he escaped, and twice was apprehended and sent back. His third attempt succeeded and Vidocq returned to Paris where he lived among brigands, thieves, and safecrackers, studying their methods and way of life. The first thing he learned about his new friends and—incidentally—about himself was that society would not allow them to earn an honest living. Any sojourn in prison, no matter how brief, became in fact a life sentence, because of a document known as a *passeport*. Everyone was required to carry this proof of identity even if merely journeying from one département of France to another. Every employer demanded to see it before he would hire even the lowliest workman. And the *passeports* of men who had served time in prison were yellow, thereby labeling their owners as ex-convicts. The hopelessness of this situation haunted Vidocq, and being audacious as well as enterprising, he faced the problem boldly. He went to the police and proposed a bargain; in return for a personal pardon, he offered his services. He would use his knowledge of the criminal world to apprehend criminals, he would form his own police force—use a thief to catch a thief. The police were delighted, for they had been unable to control a wave of crime that had been mounting steadily ever since the Revolution. (Napoleon and Josephine had been robbed twice, at the Tuileries Palace and at Saint-Cloud.)

Vidocq's men, soon known as "La Bande à Vidocq," formed France's first detective force, and developed into what is today known as the Sûreté.

Acquainted with everyone in the underworld, Vidocq also came to know the important men in the worlds of government and law enforcement, all of whom had great respect for his ability and resourcefulness. Contact with hardened criminals condemned to death led to his acquaintance with Henri Sanson; an interest in social welfare and the rehabilitation of criminals brought him to Benjamin Appert, who frequently helped the ex-convict by finding jobs for thieves and safecrackers anxious to earn an honest living.

When the demonstration ended, several of the Englishmen expressed a desire to talk further with Henri Sanson, and Appert invited the executioner to dinner. Appert notes that in accepting his invitation, Henri Sanson added rather timidly: "My son, who often replaces me on the scaffold, would be thrilled to receive the same honor."

There were several dinners at Benjamin Appert's villa in Neuilly. At the first one, the philanthropist played host to Vidocq, the Sansons (father and son), Lord Ellice, Sir John Bowring, Lord Durham, and the writers Honoré de Balzac and Alexandre Dumas. Appert apparently considered inviting Victor Hugo to this gathering but decided against it, apprehensive as to what might happen if Hugo were asked to sit down at the table with the man he had execrated in *Le Dernier Jour d'un condamné*. Balzac was embarrassed and said little or nothing, his head bent

[213]

over his plate, but Vidocq, quite at ease, chattered gaily about his own life, while the Sansons, intimidated by the titled Englishmen, sat in stony silence. Henri finally confessed his awe to Appert. Overhearing the execution-er's whisper, Vidocq laughed, saying: "He's a good fellow, is Monsieur Sanson, but I must confess it seems strange to be sitting at the same table with him."

The Englishmen began to question Henri, and even-tually he managed to conquer his shyness and answer their queries. "When I succeeded to the title of execu-tioner," Henri said at last, "my father told me that I would live in peace, and that no one would have the right to meddle in my affairs."

"Your father should have added, 'except for those whose throats you cut,' " was Vidocq's quick riposte.

At the second dinner, Appert entertained Balzac, Dumas, François-Marie-Charles Fourrier, socialist and reformer, his disciple Victor Considérant, Harel the phrenologist, and Chapelain, a doctor and hypnotist. Also present were Vidocq and the Sansons, as well as Appert's personal physician and friend, Casimir Brous-sais. The dinner was cooked by a chef named Gillard.

Appert must have had a macabre sense of humor: his chef had been arrested and sentenced to five years' imprisonment for robbery and murder (mistakenly, to be sure). He had narrowly escaped the guillotine, and had been released from prison only through the intervention of Appert, who believed him innocent and obtained a pardon from Louis-Philippe. "I had at my table," says Appert, "the *bourreau* who might have cut off the head of the innocent Gillard . . . who was that very day in my kitchen preparing dinner. All the guests were interested in Gillard's story, and asked me to have him join us for coffee to assure him of our belief in his innocence. He

[Gillard] was so affected by this confidence in him, that the tears ran down his cheeks. The two executioners were absolutely stupefied, and stared at Gillard as if they had already executed an innocent man."

This time both Balzac and Dumas carried on a lively conversation with the Sansons, their timidity as well as the Sansons' shyness having vanished. "I am overcome with sorrow when I receive my orders," said Henri-Clément, when asked how he felt on the scaffold. "And I am vastly relieved when it is all over and done with. But what can I do; it is our duty, and they [the victims] are villainous scoundrels; my father, in the case of those poor men of La Rochelle . . . felt as desolate and as unhappy as I did."

His father, Henri Sanson, was overwhelmed; he, the executioner of Paris, ordinarily shunned and despised by those of his own social milieu no less than by those of greater standing in the community, suddenly found himself dining with famous men of letters, with titled Englishmen, all of whom not only treated him as an equal, but listened to his words with respect. What could he do to show his appreciation and gratitude? Turning to his host, he offered the most valuable gift that was his to give. Appert makes no comment on the pathetic and naïve gesture, he merely reports it: "He offered me the clothing of the condemned, the clothing of those whose trials cause the most furor and notoriety. That is how I came to possess the redingotes of Fieschi, of Lacenaire, of Alibaud. . . . It was one of Sanson's valets who brought me these things, and I always gave him fifteen francs for the *cadeau* so that he should not be out of pocket, for these sad vestments meant income for the valet."

Although there was no prejudice against the executioner in the house of Benjamin Appert, he confirms the

[215]

fact that it still existed. "However," he adds, "it is no longer universal, because no sooner does a position of this kind become vacant, than that same day the Ministry receives hundreds of applications, and the relatives of the dead man do not hesitate to claim *droits du sang* . . . blood rights. As it is extremely rare that the sons of an executioner are able to find other employment, many believe that the law compels a son to follow in his father's footsteps. This is not true, but the advantages of doing so are sufficiently great so that sons accept their heritage."

In 1828–1830 Balzac is reputed to have written and edited (in collaboration with an impecunious writer named Lhéritier de l'Ain) a work entitled *Mémoires pour servir à l'histoire de la Révolution Française, par Sanson, Executeur des Arrets criminels pendant la Révolution.* He did not in fact write any part of this fictitious work except for the introduction, which was published in 1842 under his name in the *Royal Keepsake*, again in 1845 under the title of *Une Messe en 1793*, and subsequently in his *Comédie Humaine, Scènes de la Vie Politique*, in a chapter called "Un Épisode sous la Terreur." Nor had Balzac ever interviewed Henri Sanson for the purpose of collecting information about his father. A letter unearthed by Roger Goulard, and published in the *Mercure de France* in November of 1950, reveals that Marco de Saint-Hilaire, a childhood friend of Balzac's, had done the research for the alleged memoirs of Charles-Henri Sanson, and that it was Saint-Hilaire who interviewed the executioner. "I learned a great many things . . . from the Père Sanson [Henri]," says Saint-Hilaire, "because I saw him often, and because aside from his job, he was a very nice person, who played the bass viol extremely badly, but was an excellent *père de famille*. . . . In his tulip garden, accompanied by his gray parrot who followed him like a little dog,

[216]

he told me all about the executions he had performed during and after the Revolution."

Balzac's sister, Madame Laure Surville, confirms the fact that the writer's introduction to Messieurs Sanson took place at Benjamin Appert's, and that he obtained the information for *Un Épisode sous la Terreur* from the executioner himself.

> My brother wanted to see Samson, [she reports, in *Balzac, sa Vie et ses Oeuvres d'après sa corréspondance*]. He wanted to know the thoughts of this man whose soul was so filled with bloody memories, learn how he felt about his terrible function, his miserable life; this was a project that intrigued him.
>
> M.A. . . . [Appert] . . . director of Prisons, with whom my brother was friendly, arranged the meeting. Honoré discovered, one day at M.A.'s house, a pale-faced man with a countenance both noble and sad; his dress his manner, his language, his education were those of a scholar . . . this scholar was Samson! . . . My brother, warned by M.A. . . . repressed his astonishment, his revulsion, and turned the conversation to subjects that interested him. He was so successful in winning the confidence of Samson that the man was drawn into revealing the suffering he had endured. The death of Louis XVI had left him filled with the terror and the remorse of a criminal. (Samson was a royalist.) On the morning following the execution, he had a mass said for the King, probably the only expiatory mass said in Paris on that day. . . .

Both Balzac and Dumas would use Vidocq, the

reformed criminal, in their writings—his traits, characteristics, even some episodes from his life. Vautrin, Balzac's fictitious character who, like Vidocq, was first a criminal and then a policeman, appears in *Le Père Goriot*, in *La Dernière Incarnation de Vautrin*, in *La Cousine Bette*, and in other novels of the *Comédie Humaine*. Vidocq's likeness appears in Alexandre Dumas's *Gabriel Lambert*; and the man so deeply affected by problems of crime and punishment would use Vidocq in his powerful novel *Les Misérables*. Jean Valjean in Victor Hugo's *chef d'oeuvre* is modeled on François-Eugène Vidocq.

Benjamin Appert's dinners, which brought Hugo, Balzac, and Dumas together with the Sansons and Vidocq, left deep wounds on all three writers. All would cry out against the terrible conditions in French prisons, the injustice of a society made for the rich and powerful, and the death sentence itself, which they looked upon as cruel, needless, and wasteful.

> One is sometimes tempted to believe that defenders of the death penalty haven't really thought about what it means, [wrote Hugo]. Consider for a moment a crime, any crime; compare it to this outrageous right arrogated by the state of taking that which it has not given, consider this punishment, the most irreparable of all irreparable punishments.
>
> The man we punish may be without family, without relatives, without friends in this world. In that case he has received neither education, nor teaching, nor concern for his mind or his heart; by what right do we kill this unhappy orphan? We · punish him for a childhood that forced him to cling to the earth without roots and without help!

We make him pay for the loneliness to which we consigned him! Of his misfortune we create a crime! No one taught him to realize what he was doing. The man knows nothing. His fault is caused by destiny, not himself. We punish an innocent.

Perhaps this man has a family; do we believe that the blow we inflict wounds him alone? that his father, his mother, his children will not bleed? No. In killing him we decapitate the entire family. And here again, we punish the innocent.

. . . This man, this guilty one with a family, isolate him. In prison he will be able to work for his loved ones. But how can he support them from the grave?

May the most obstinate criminologists hear my words; for a century capital punishment has been decreasing. Today it is almost rare. Evidence of decrepitude. Evidence of weakness. Evidence of its future demise. Torture has been abolished, the wheel has disappeared, the gallows is no more. Strange fact, the guillotine is progress.

To those who regret the passing of the gods, one can say God is here. To those who regret the passing of kings, one can say the country still exists. To those who will regret the executioner, there is nothing to say.

Order will not disappear with the executioner. Do not believe this. The vault of future society will not crumble without this hideous keystone.

The gentle law of Christ will ultimately penetrate the Code of laws and shine through it. We shall look upon crime as an illness, and this illness will have its doctors to replace judges, its hospitals to replace the galleys. . . .

[219]

If the campaign initiated by Hugo and heightened by the work of Benjamin Appert did not succeed in its attempt to abolish capital punishment, it must have given the Sansons, father and son, some worrisome moments. Hugo wrote that "The scaffold is the only edifice that revolutions fail to demolish." But because of his efforts and those of others, it had been shaken to its foundations.

Despite discussions and debates in the Parlement, despite the writings of Hugo and his contemporaries, the guillotine continued to function. The instrument of justice had not changed since its invention, but it no longer worked at such a furious pace. Messieurs De Paris were not completely idle, however, for crimes against the state still brought the death penalty. During February of 1836 five men were found guilty of regicide and a sixth man soon thereafter.

On February 8, 1836, Lacenaire, a poet, and his accomplice Avril went to the scaffold for an attempt on the life of Louis-Philippe. Avril's execution took place without incident. But when Lacenaire lay on the *bascule,* the blade of the guillotine stuck in its groove just above the neck of its victim. Three times the poor man looked up at the blood-stained knife that had made its descent to within centimeters of his body, and three times the end did not come. The public, aroused by the fact that

Lacenaire had received the death penalty, had tried in vain to have his sentence commuted, so that this final indignity, this needless agony caused more furor than usual. Nor did the press spare the executioner in reporting *l'incident du couteau.* Despite Henri-Clément's written protests, no newspaper would publish his statement that "nothing out-of-the-way had occurred when Lacenaire met his death, which was enacted with no more difficulty than that of his accomplice, Avril."

Public opinion had changed since July 25, 1794, when another poet and revolutionary, André Chenier, had gone to the guillotine for his protests against the Reign of Terror. Concern for the life of a human being had shown itself at last—in the public press.

On Monday, July 27, 1835, a tradesman named Joseph Suireau presented himself at the Commissariat de Police and reported that on the 28th, during a celebration scheduled to commemorate the fifth anniversary of the 1830 Revolution, an attempt would be made on the life of Louis-Philippe. Informed of the rumor, the King waved it aside, stubbornly refusing to call off the festivities, which had already been postponed from May 1st to this July date.

Immense crowds lined the route of the royal cortège. The boulevards and side streets were packed with spectators, both royalist and revolutionary. Flags hung from balconies and flew from rooftops. Mothers held their children high in the air so that they could see the parade, catch a glimpse of the King as he rode by. But an explosion cut through the cheering; the King's horse reared as a bullet went through its ear. The maréchal Mortier, duc de Trevise, fell to the ground, killed instantly, and over fifty people were injured in the blast. Unharmed, Louis-Philippe was rushed to the Tuileries palace, while his wounded officers lay bleeding and while a young woman died in her father's arms.

The man responsible for this terrible explosion was trapped by the King's men while trying to escape, confessed proudly to having perpetrated the crime, and was imprisoned in the Conciergerie. A forty-six-year-old Corsican by the name of Giuseppe Marco Fieschi, he had served in the army under Murat, then returned to the island of his birth where he served ten years in prison for theft and forgery. At the expiration of his sentence he traveled to Paris, but in spite of forged papers and *passeport*, he was unable to find employment. Believing himself a victim of tyranny, filled with bitterness and self-pity, he swore revenge on the society that had treated him so ungratefully. And, as misery usually finds its own level, Fieschi found his in an organization called the Société des Droits de l'Homme, one of a number of revolutionary groups that flourished in Paris during this period.

There he had met Theodore-Florentin Pépin, thin and lanky, a grocer who had been a member of the National Guard during the Revolution of 1789 and despised the royalist regime. Pépin introduced Fieschi to a friend named Morey, a great admirer of Marat and Robespierre, and Morey managed to get the indigent Corsican a job. One evening when the three had gathered for a drink, Fieschi showed his friends the design of a weapon, variously described as having had twenty, twenty-five, and according to some reports fifty rifles mounted on a wooden framework and rigged so that they would all fire at once. Fieschi called his invention the *machine infernale* and together the three revolutionaries discussed its possibilities and hatched their plot.

They ascertained the exact route to be taken by

[222]

Louis-Philippe; they then rented an apartment on the third floor of a house at 50 boulevard du Temple with windows overlooking the wide street along which the parade would pass. On the 15th of April Fieschi moved into his new abode and began assembling wood for the framework of his cannon. On May 1st he learned that the parade had been postponed. When the day finally arrived, he fired off his machine, but when the machine exploded its gigantic charge, he was horribly wounded. He tried to escape via an inner courtyard of the building, but his bloodied appearance no less than his furtive movements soon led to capture—and the naming of his accomplices.

The trial of the three men began on February 1, 1836; on February 18th the verdict was rendered—all three were condemned to death. During the night of February 19–20, Henri Sanson and his son and their aides set up the scaffold at the Rond Point de la Barrière Saint-Jacques. Once again, they were made to feel the public's wrath. Enraged by the slaughter of innocent spectators during the parade, men and women, royalist and revolutionary alike, thronged the area, their anger directed at the miscreants and at the executioner. The authorities finally had to send a troop of cavalry to patrol the streets so that the scaffold could be assembled and made ready.

The day of the execution dawned cold and blustery. Henri Sanson, noticing that Fieschi wore only pants and vest, asked the prisoner whether he wouldn't feel the cold without an overcoat. Fieschi, proud of his vengeful deed and eager for martyrdom, turned on the executioner. "Bah," he sneered. "I shall be a lot colder when they bury me."

When the guillotine's blade had come down for the third time, the crowd, almost all of it anti-royalist in

[223]

sentiment, surged forward in an attempt to seize the clothing of the criminals, the ropes that bound their wrists, locks of their hair. Henri-Clément, in a desperate move to protect his father and himself, threw Pépin and Morey's effects to the mob; but not until the police had come to their assistance could the two Sansons make their escape.

The sixth victim of the guillotine, another regicide, went to his death without fanfare or incident. Remembering the ugly horde that had fought its way to the scaffold after the execution of Fieschi, the gendarmerie was out in force. But less than fifty people appeared to witness the death of Alibaud, whose bullets had gone wide of their mark, harming no one.

Henri-Clément, whose natural pallor was accentuated by the somber black of his everyday attire, had become a familiar figure on the scaffold during the third decade of the nineteenth century. Parisians knew him as well if not better than his ailing father. It was common gossip that whether he took part in an execution or merely observed the proceedings, ugly red blotches mottled his ashen countenance and his entire body was racked by violent trembling. "No one is more miserable than I," the young man confessed quite openly. "When I receive my orders to perform an execution, I become feverish."

The death of Henri Sanson in August of 1840 brought Henri-Clément the title of executioner. For months he deliberated, dreamed of leaving the profession of his ancestors, freeing himself of the intolerable yoke. But at the age of forty-one, what else could he do to earn a living? He knew no other trade. And so on December 1st, when he received formal notification of his appointment, he shrugged his shoulders: the die had been cast long before his birth. But from that moment on, he began to exhibit all the characteristics of a trapped animal. The profession he had loathed since childhood, the profession which was for him a life sentence, had become unbearable, and like many prisoners he began searching for ways to escape. A natural taste for luxury grew to exaggerated proportions, as if he could blot the hated profession out of existence by spending money on horses and fancy carriages, collecting paintings, having his suits made by the most expensive tailors, excessive drinking and card-playing. He frequented houses of ill-repute, he gambled, his losses so great that his wife became alarmed and pleaded with him to stop. But the unhappy man ignored the warnings of relatives and friends. He had been denied the right to choose his life-work, but no one could deny him the right to escape when he so desired.

It was during this difficult period of his life that he decided to renovate the house, removing the iron grill-work and replacing it with an elegant oak doorway and adding the glassed-in veranda, as if the changes in outer appearances could lighten the darkness within himself. Unmindful, indifferent, oblivious to expenditures of money that were increasing at an alarming pace, Henri-Clément not only left as much of his work as he dared to his aides, but gave up the practice of medicine. As a result, the family fortune which Henri had carefully built

[225]

up and husbanded was rapidly vanishing. (The twelve thousand francs paid to the executioner had been reduced to eight thousand in 1832. In 1849 it would be cut again.)

Henri-Clément's excesses were a constant source of concern and an increasing cause of friction in the household—which like that of his father and grandfather was a large one, sheltering impoverished relatives, his father's widow, his servants and aides. His wife had borne three children, but only two of them remained. The son (and only boy) was killed in infancy in a carriage accident near Brunoy. In 1837, the older of the girls, Marie-Emilie, born in 1818, married Jean-Nicolas Jouënne, surgeon at the military hospital in Perpignan, son and grandson of the executioners of Melun. The Jouënnes came from a long line of executioners, one of whom had married the first Charles Sanson, others having plied their trade in Caen, Caudebec-en-Caux, Arras, Evreux, Le Mans, Rouen, and Dieppe. The children of this marriage, Marie-Henriette and Paul-Louis, grew up on the Ile Saint-Louis in Paris, where their father practiced medicine. Henri-Clément's grandchildren were a source of great pride to him, and he liked to boast that his daughter had married outside of the confrèrie. In 1845, the younger daughter, Thérèse-Clémentine-Antoinette married Théodore-Joseph Clarisse, a clerk, and it is known that following her husband's death, she retired to a convent. (She died in 1912 at the age of eighty-five.)

In 1844, James Rousseau, the editor of the *Gazette des Tribunaux*, published an account of his visit to the Sanson household in the rue des Marais just prior to Henri's death. He describes the old executioner as "a man who appeared to be about sixty years old, but was actually seventy; with a frank, open countenance and an expression that was both gentle and calm. His height, his marvelous bald head, and his regular features gave him the look of a patriarch." He adds that Henri Sanson made no attempt to conceal his distaste for the job in which fate had placed him. He bore it not as a man who scorned the consequences, but as a wise soul who knew his own worth, who understood that a man can always raise himself above the level of his birth regardless of his profession. But Rousseau also found traces of a deference verging on servility, an awareness of the distance that separated a *bourreau* from other men. As an example he cites the fact that Henri used snuff but did not offer any to his guest. When in the course of conversation Rousseau drew out his own *tabatière* and held it out to the executioner, Henri recoiled; the bloodstained fingers of a *bourreau* were not supposed to touch the possessions of others. A second incident occurred as Rousseau was leaving; he held out his hand, only to see his host step back, an expression of astonishment mingled with horror contorting his face. An executioner, at least during the *ancien régime*, never touched the person of others—except for his victims. And Henri still retained old habits and old customs.

"The present executioner [Henri-Clément] is quite different from his father," says Rousseau. "In speaking of his profession and the details involved, he exhibits none of the hesitation, none of the constraint, none of the *malaise* of the older man. Convinced of the necessity of his office and of the service he renders to society, he considers himself no more than a bailiff carrying out orders, and he speaks of his function with amazing freedom." One cannot help but wonder if Rousseau had not mistaken freedom for bravado, if Henri-Clément's attitude had not

[227]

deceived the journalist completely, if the young executioner, suspecting that his words would appear in print, had bluffed—and won.

Upon learning that Henri-Clément's daughter had married a physician, the journalist expressed his astonishment. He quotes Henri-Clément's reply: "To save a human being, a surgeon is frequently obliged to cut off a diseased limb," said the executioner. "The same can be said of society."

"May I suggest," said the journalist, "that between the two there is quite a difference."

"Only in the dimensions of the knife," was the answer. In what tone of voice did Henri-Clément utter these words? What lift of the eyebrow, what twist of the lip accompanied them?

Rousseau, who visited the Sansons more than once, observed that:

> Since the death of Henri Sanson, the little house in the rue des Marais has lost its weird, lugubrious air. The rusted iron grille has given way to one of those elegant doorways . . . in the courtyard, which is quite large, a sort of glassed-in and domed projection has been added, the interior of which forms an elegant vestibule. To the left of this vestibule are the kitchen, the pantry, and the service quarters; to the right of it, the dining room and a small salon where Monsieur de Paris receives his visitors. On the first floor are the bedrooms to which guests are not admitted, and where Madame Sanson keeps herself. In all of my visits both to father and to son, I have never seen her. What I have seen of the house is furnished with a severe simplicity suitable to such a dwelling.

If Madame Sanson kept to herself, it was because the marriage was not a happy one. The former Virginie-Emilie Lefébure would ultimately leave her husband and go to live with her daughter, Madame Jouënne, on the Île Saint-Louis, remaining there from about 1847 until her death in 1860.

While Henri-Clément drank and gambled and left most of his duties to his first assistant Piot, France itself was growing tired of the July Monarchy. Legitimist followers of Charles X sat in the rotting splendor of their mansions in the faubourg Saint-Germain and moaned the passing of privilege. The Church, excluded from teaching in the schools, opposed a King who supported godless institutions. Young republicans discussed and yearned to emulate the glories of the past, socialists put forth plans for a communist society, and Bonapartists made snide comparisons between the victories of their Emperor and the mediocre, do-nothing government of Louis-Philippe. The French were impatient with the status quo, eager and ready for change. The inauguration of the Arc de Triomphe in 1836 and the raising of the obelisk of Luxor in the place de la Concorde (erstwhile place de la Révolution) recalled proud memories of Napoleon's *Grande Armée*. When in 1840 the ashes of the Emperor were brought back from Saint Helena and placed beneath the dome of the Invalides, republican zeal joined forces with socialist dreams and a new fusion party was born. The populace responded to this atmosphere of change and revealed itself more than receptive to new ideas, more than ready for the revolution that was rapidly taking shape. On ground as fertile as this, a campaign for the abolition of capital punishment would gain momentum, bringing with it further

[229]

and said to her: "We call it *enfourner*. [Literally, to put in the oven.]

"Well, Monsieur Sanson," said the young girl, "I want you to put me in the oven."

The *bourreau* winced. He protested. The young girl insisted. "I want to be able to say that I was tied down on that thing," she said.

Sanson looked at her parents. They replied: "If that is what she wants, do it."

He had to give in. The *bourreau* made the young miss sit down, he bound her legs together with rope, he tied her arms behind her back, he laid her on the *bascule* and buckled the leather strap around her body. He wanted to stop there.

"No, no, you haven't finished," she protested.

Sanson leveled the *bascule,* put the young girl's head in the *lunette,* and closed its two halves together. Only then was she content.

Later, in telling the story, Sanson said, "I was waiting for the moment when she would say 'You still haven't finished. Let the blade fall.' "

Almost all English visitors asked to see the blade that cut off the head of Louis XVI. That blade had been sold for scrap iron, just as all other blades were sold when they became too old and too dull for use. The English didn't believe this and offered to buy the blade. If he had wanted to make money, he could have sold as many *couteaux de Louis XVI* as the so-called *cannes de Voltaire.*

As it happened, Henri-Clément did sell the blade that had decapitated the King, but under different circumstances, and just about a year after this account was published.

The executioner's morale sank lower and lower, despite the infrequency of his visits to the scaffold. To bolster it, he spent more and more time in gambling houses, bought more expensive paintings and furniture for his house, and lavished more presents on women until one day he awakened to the fact that his debts exceeded his ability to pay. He began pawning objets d'art and family possessions in order to pay his creditors, but by this time there were too many creditors, too much of a gap between what he could realize and what he owed. The threat of Clichy, the prison for debtors (so-named because of its location on the rue de Clichy) had become a reality.

Paris prisons, such as the Conciergerie, La Force, Sainte-Pélagie, the Luxembourg, the Châtelet (almost eighty of them existed during the Revolution) varied, both as to the character of those imprisoned and the accommodation given them. The Conciergerie, situated near the Seine, was known to be the worst. Beaulieu, editor of the *Courrier Français* who was incarcerated as an alleged "suspect," described it as "the most horrible, the most pernicious of all. . . . One waited for a room with a bed for as long as fifteen days; one paid eighteen francs a month for such accommodation. When the river was high, it reached the level of the prison floor, and then humidity prevailed everywhere; water streamed down every wall." Dukes and princes shared cells with robbers and murderers, slept on pallets of vermin-infested straw, and were treated in the same brutal way whether sentenced for murder or merely for speaking out against the regime.

In strong contrast to the Conciergerie, Clichy housed neither murderers nor political prisoners. No disgrace was attached to a term of imprisonment for debt; in fact, some of its inmates bore the most distinguished names in

France. Clichy offered large, airy, completely furnished rooms, not cells; and the rooms were not only clean and comfortable but heated. The prison provided a library, a post office, and messengers to run errands in Paris for any prisoner who had need of such service. Recreation took place in the prison courtyard, where men enjoyed a game of skittles and women could walk about. Relatives and friends were permitted to visit the unfortunates, and to send them food and drink.

Unlike ordinary criminals, debtors were escorted to Clichy by men known as *recors* (process servers), rather than by gendarmes of the Paris police. The *recors* were forbidden by law to apprehend a victim outside of Paris, and to make their task more difficult, the arrest had to be effected between six o'clock in the evening and six in the morning. As a consequence, men pursued by their creditors made it a habit to leave Paris for one of the suburbs during the daylight hours, sneaking back at twilight to see their loved ones and sleep in their own beds. Henri-Clément soon found himself among these fugitives who spent their days drinking, eating, and playing cards in local taverns and cafés, one ear cocked for the striking of the clock that would signal their nightly release.

For several months, Monsieur de Paris managed to elude capture, thanks to the leniency of the courts, which during a fairly lengthy period sent no one to the guillotine. But the day came when Henri-Clément received his orders for another execution.

Another regicide had been sentenced to death, a man named Lecomte, erstwhile member of the *Légion d'Honneur* and chief forester of the royal domain of Fontainbleau. Reprimanded and fined for brutality to his subordinates on more than one occasion, he finally resigned his job and claimed a pension. But the forest of Fontainbleau was a private domain which belonged to the King but not to the Crown. And as a private employee, Lecomte was not entitled to a pension. The angry *Garde Générale de la Forêt* wrote to Louis-Philippe three times, without receiving an answer. At last, furious at being so abused and mistreated, Lecomte resolved to kill the man who had so injured him. Stationing himself on top of a wall near the château, he waited until Louis-Philippe, accompanied by his wife and grandchildren, appeared in the palace driveway in an open carriage. When two bursts from his gun failed to hit any member of the royal entourage, Lecomte ran into the forest, where he was quickly captured.

The Chamber of Peers debated his case for five days, and thirty-two members voted the death penalty. The thirty-third man who got to his feet was Victor Hugo.

"For eighteen years I have had definite and comprehensive ideas on the subject of capital punishment," said Hugo, who had been elected to the Chamber only the year before. "You are familiar with these ideas. As a mere writer, I have published them. As a politician, with God's help I shall apply them. In general, capital punishment is repulsive to me, I cannot accept it. Pierre Lecomte, a lonely, wretched man, would of necessity become ferocious, disturbed in spirit. His attempt upon the life of the King, an attempt upon a father at a time when he was surrounded by his family, an attempt upon a group of women and children . . . the crime is monstrous. Now let us examine the motive: twenty francs withheld from his salary (of three hundred), his resignation accepted, three letters written which were never answered, how could he help but be stricken by such a combination, by such an abyss. . . . Faced with these two

[235]

extremes, the most serious crime and the most trifling motive, it is quite plain to me that there is a lack of reason, and that this guilty man, this assassin, this savage and lonely man, this frightened and ferocious being is insane. I vote for life imprisonment."

Two other members of the Chamber joined Hugo, but with 229 votes against him, Lecomte was sentenced to death.

On June 8, 1846, Henri-Clément ascended the scaffold and directed the procedings, then accompanied the body of the deceased to the cemetery of Clamart before returning to his house in the rue des Marais. Had he been aware of the process-server who dogged his footsteps throughout the day? He'd have had a difficult time avoiding the *recors,* whose carriage followed his every move. That evening, Henri-Clément Sanson was taken to Clichy prison, where despite his protests, he remained for some time.

And then he had an inspiration. He would pawn the guillotine. The instrument was his, why not use it to pay his creditors? Accompanied by the *recors,* he was permitted to leave Clichy and to go to the quai de Valmy where he kept his machine. From there he took it to his principal creditor, who promised to return it to him when he had paid his debt, amounting to 3,800 francs.

Several months passed, months during which time Henri-Clément must have held his breath, for if an order to execute had arrived at his door, he would have been unable to carry it out. Such orders usually came the day before the event, so that the *bourreau* and his aides would have time to set up the scaffold and make their preparations. On March 17, 1847, the papers were delivered, bidding the executioner of Criminal Judgments of the City of Paris to present himself at the Palais de Justice at such-and-such a time. Henri-Clément pleaded with his creditor to release the guillotine, even if just for the morning, to no avail. Finally he had to present himself at the Ministry of Justice and confess his predicament. The Minister had no choice but to order payment of 3,800 francs to Henri-Clément Sanson, so that he could redeem his machine. On June 18th, he guillotined his last victim, and that evening he received notice of his dismissal.

The last of the Sansons had come to the end of his career.

Henri-Clément at forty-eight found him- self alone (his wife had left him), without means of support—unemployed and unemployable. His house, put up for sale by his creditors, was bought by a leather worker named Edouard Plouvier, who made and sold the straps for the *bascule* of the guillotine. The former executioner and his mother retired to the country, not to the property in Brunoy, which had also been sold to pay his debts, but to some small village where they lived quietly and no doubt simply, while the Revolution of 1848 ushered in the Second Republic. "But for the advanced age and the infirmities of my mother," wrote Henri-Clément, "I should have journeyed to the New World. . . . America with its new ways, its virgin forests, its immense rivers, of which I had read in the works of Chateaubriand and Fenimore Cooper, was the land I longed to see." His financial condition being what it was, it is doubtful that this statement contains anything more than wishful thinking.

There were eighteen applicants for the job of Monsieur de Paris, a fact that is scarcely surprising in view of the number of provincial executioners who had been dismissed from their posts during the preceding decades. Joseph Heinderech, son of the executioner of Mâcon, won the coveted title which had by now become the only secure post within the confrèrie.

A decree of March 1849 further diminished the number of *bourreaux;* henceforth there would be one executioner for each provincial Court of Appeal, said executioner to reside in the town in which the court was located. The same decree suppressed all aides, except for two in the département of the Seine (Paris) and one in Corsica. Salaries shrank: five thousand francs for Monsieur de Paris, four thousand in Lyon, three thousand each in Bordeaux and Toulouse.

That same year, in the epilogue of Dumas's play *Comte Hermann,* which the author says in his *Mémoires* was intended to be read and not acted, he writes:

> Twenty years ago, the death penalty was effected in the center of Paris at the busiest hour of the day, in front of the greatest possible number of spectators. . . . Today it is no longer performed in that fashion; one step has been taken toward the abolition of capital punishment in transporting the instrument of death almost beyond the city limits, in choosing an hour which for the majority of Parisians is still an hour of sleep, and in furnishing for the guilty man's last minutes only that rare witness which chance or excessive curiosity has drawn to the scaffold.

Now it is up to the priests devoted to the well-being of the condemned to tell us if they find as many hard hearts in the journey that leads from Bicêtre to the Barrière Saint-Jacques as they found in the trip from the Conciergerie to the place de Grève, if there are as many tears shed today at four o'clock in the morning at the foot of the crucifix as there were at four o'clock in the evening.

We believe it fervently.

Yes, there will be more repentance in silence and meditation than there was in tumult and crowds.

And now let us suppose that the execution, removed from the curious eyes of the public which learns nothing from it nor is bettered by it, but which is only hardened to the sight of death; suppose that the execution takes place in a prison, witnessed only by the priest and the executioner . . . suppose that the execution is performed by electricity, which kills like a thunderbolt, or by a poisonous drug which induces sleep; will not the heart of the condemned man be softened to an even greater degree in this night, in this silence, in this solitude, than it would be in the light of day. . . . Executions are now performed in front of the gates of the Prison de la Roquette. From there to executing within the prison is only a matter of a few steps.

And to descend from the courtyard of the prison to the cell itself is only one step.

The next step, insofar as the executioners were concerned, occurred on June 26, 1850, when a decree cut their salaries again. This time Monsieur de Paris received only four thousand francs, his confrères in the provinces three thousand and two thousand.

On June 18th of the same year, Marie-Louise Damidot, Henri Sanson's widow died, leaving Henri-Clément alone in his country retreat, "a place so safe and so secluded that nothing could ever remind me of the melancholy occupation of my former life," he wrote, confessing however, that although he lived under an assumed name, he lived in constant fear that his new friends and neighbors would discover his true identity.

In 1857 he returned to Paris, where it is believed he bought a house on the outskirts of the city; whether with funds saved from his mother's pension, or with money obtained from his father-in-law's estate (his wife died in 1860) history does not relate.

Meanwhile, the Second Republic, eager to shed the mediocrity and dullness of Louis-Philippe, had elected as its President Louis Napoleon Bonaparte, a nephew of Napoleon, and (through the death of Napoleon's son) heir to the imperial succession. His military *coup d'état* of December 2, 1851, caused the Republic to give way to a Second Empire, which was promptly accepted by a majority of French voters. The decade between 1850 and 1860 was a prosperous one. Due to improved methods of manufacture and swifter transport, industry expanded, prices for commodities rose in the world markets, employment was high. Baron Haussmann's beautification of Paris turned twisting streets into broad avenues, cul-de-sacs into proud squares. An exposition in 1855 informed visitors from all over Europe that Paris was once again the gay, elegant city it had been under Louis XIV and Napoleon Bonaparte. The fashionable and lovely Empress Eugénie presided over a court that was dazzling in its splendor, and Frenchmen held their heads high, boasting that their nation led the world in the arts, in fashion—and in grandeur.

But like his ancestor, Napoleon III needed wars to enhance his prestige: in 1854 France joined Britain in the Crimean conflict. In 1859 Napoleon III attempted to expel the Austrians from Italy, and in 1870 the Franco-Prussian war exploded. The surrender of the French forces at Sedan in September saw the fall of the Empire and the creation of the Third Republic. The remaining decades of the nineteenth century would be peaceful ones, however, not only for France but for all of Europe; and in periods of peace, nations can turn their thoughts to themselves and their domestic problems. One of the Third Republic's first decrees would involve the executioner.

On November 25, 1870, all executioners were eliminated save one: he would reside in Paris, and be allowed five aides, also resident in the capital city. Monsieur de Paris would receive six thousand francs a year, two of his aides four thousand each, and three aides three thousand. Two guillotines were to be maintained in Paris and transported to whatever locality might need them. Louis Deibler, erstwhile assistant to Joseph Heinderech, received the title of executioner for France and Algeria. His son Anatole would succeed him.

Henri-Clément spent his declining years with his older daughter Marie-Emilie Jouënne in Versailles, where Madame Jouënne, herself a widow, earned a modest living by teaching. Her father, known to the neighbors as Monsieur Henri, lived to see the Exposition of 1888 and to marvel at the Eiffel Tower which formed part of it. But he did not live to celebrate the 100th anniversary of the Revolution, on July 14, 1889. He died on the 25th of January, six months before it would take place, in his

[241]

ninetieth year, and was buried in the cemetery of Montmartre.

Just two years after Henri-Clément's death, a book was published entitled *Là-Bas* (*Down There*). Its author, Joris-Karl Huysmans (1848–1907), whose writings were a mixture of Zola's realism and Baudelaire's decadence, pictures the executioner as viewed through the eyes of the late nineteenth century, an era when many writers and artists were preoccupied with and fascinated by mysticism, satanism, deterioration, and death:

> It is quite certain that in this more than in any previous century, the nerves quiver at the least shock. For instance, recall the newspaper accounts of executions of criminals. We learn that the executioner goes about his work timidly, that he is on the point of fainting, that he has nervous prostration when he decapitates a man. Then compare this nervous wreck with the invincible torturers of olden time. They would thrust your arm into a sleeve of moistened parchment which when set on fire would draw up and in a leisurely fashion reduce your flesh to dust. Or they would drive wedges into your thighs and split the bones. They would crush your thumbs in the thumbscrew. Or they would singe all the hair off your epidermis with a poker, or roll up the skin from your abdomen and leave you with a kind of apron. They would drag you at the cart's tail, give you the strappado, roast you, drench you with ignited alcohol, and through it all preserve an impassive countenance and tranquil nerves not to be shaken by any cry or plaint. Only, as these exercises were somewhat fatiguing, the torturers, after the operation, were ravenously hungry and

required a great deal to drink. They were
sanguinaries of a mental stability not to be
shaken. . . .

How fortunate that the last, and most sensitive,
member of the Sanson family did not live to read these
words. When they appeared, in 1891, he had been
granted the escape that he and his ancestors had granted
to so many others.

Henri-Clément's granddaughter, Thérèse-Clémentine-
Antoinette Clarisse, looked after the modest tombstone
for many years; and every year on the 21st of January,
the anniversary of Louis XVI's death, she was seen by
the guardians of the cemetery, placing an armful of
flowers on the grave of her ancestors. In 1920 she retired
to a convent near Poitiers, and the Sanson family, having
performed its macabre function for seven generations,
faded into history.

The invention of Joseph-Ignace Guillotin,
first used on a human being in 1792, is still in use today.
And as of this writing, there is still a Monsieur de Paris.

Louis Anatole Stanislas Deibler, who succeeded to the
post at the time of the Franco-Prussian war, executed 169
criminals. His nephew Anatole, who had served as his
aide, inherited the position in 1899, and would execute
over three hundred during his tenure of office. When

Anatole died in February of 1930, his nephew by marriage, Henri Desfourneaux, acquired the title, retaining it until his own death in 1951. The current executioner, André Obrecht, is a nephew of Anatole's.

Another dynasty in the making? The seventy-three-year-old incumbent who earns $5,200 a year, and has performed 362 executions, was asked whether he knew the name of his successor. "No, I don't know who it will be," he replied. "Do you think there will be one?"

Despite Alexandre Dumas' ardent plea in 1849 that executions be performed within the prison walls, they remained public spectacles until just before World War II. On June 17, 1939, a man convicted of murder was guillotined in front of the Palais de Justice of Versailles. Throughout the night preceding his execution, Siegfried Eugen Weidmann could hear the mob converging upon the place of execution. Every room, every balcony, every window overlooking the Palais de Justice had been rented for the occasion. An account in *Le Figaro* reported that:

> Despite the rain that fell all night, the population of Versailles was not deterred from gathering on the rue Georges Clemenceau in front of the prison gates, where at about three o'clock in the morning, Monsieur Desfourneaux and his aides set up the guillotine. . . . From midnight on, a special force composed of gendarmes, militia, and inspectors of the Sûreté barred the streets leading to the Palais de Justice and the prison. A nearby café where numerous drinkers had installed themselves found the view from its terrace obscured by a large truck which parked directly in front of it to prevent the curious from staring at the place of execution.

Weidmann was guillotined just before five o'clock in the morning, in front of as bloodthirsty and unruly a mob of men and women (a great many women were present) as had gathered in the place de la Révolution one hundred and fifty years earlier.

The scene, photographed by every newspaper in France, produced such an effect that one week later, on June 24th, a decree was issued forbidding future public executions. Henceforth they would take place within the prison yard, in the presence of the presiding judge of the Assizes, an officer from the public prosecutor's office, the judge of the tribunal belonging to the district where the execution took place, the clerk of the Assizes, the defense lawyer, a minister or priest, the director of the prison, the Commissaire of police, and the prison doctor. After the execution, a placard should be affixed to the gates of the prison, announcing that the execution had taken place and giving the date and the hour.

According to the *Code Pénal*, crimes punishable by death include assassination, parricide, poisoning, murder, arson, and crimes against the state—i.e. treason, espionage, giving information to the enemy, and the inciting of civil war.

The war years in France (1940–1945) saw many executions, for espionage, for treason, for political as well as civil crimes; but the services of the state executioner during that period did not figure as prominently as those of the military. Monsieur Desfourneaux's career, however, was not without activity; one of his most notorious victims went to the guillotine in May of 1946, condemned for having killed no less than twenty-five people.

Desfourneaux died in October of 1951. One month later, on November 8th, a tiny article, buried on page

[245]

nine of *Le Figaro*, announced that his successor had been named. "Le Nouveau Monsieur de Paris est Designé," said the modest headline. "Mais Bénéficie Encore de l'Incognito. (The new Monsieur de Paris has been named but still enjoys incognito)." The article stated that, as was customary, the name of the new executioner would not be made public until such time as an execution was scheduled to take place.

In October of 1952 the question of capital punishment burst forth into headlines again. By this time twenty-one countries had abolished the death penalty (Norway, Sweden, Denmark, Finland, Iceland, Italy, Switzerland, Brazil, Argentina, Dominican Republic, Venezuela, New Zealand, Austria, West Germany, Low Countries, Belgium, Colombia, Costa Rica, Australia, San Marino, Portugal, as well as seven states in the United States). But in France, 1,465 men had been condemned to death and had perished by the guillotine in the eight years from 1944 to 1952. Victor Hugo's words to the Chamber of Deputies in 1848 appeared in print once more: "There are three things that belong to God and not to man; the irrevocable, the irreparable, the indissoluble. Woe unto man if he introduces them into his code of laws."

And in opposition, the words of Jean-Jacques Rousseau: "Every malefactor, by attacking social rights becomes on forfeit a rebel and a traitor to his country; by violating its laws he ceases to be a member of it; he even makes war upon it. In such a case the preservation of the State is inconsistent with his own, and one or the other must perish; in putting the guilty to death we slay not so much the citizen as the enemy."

From 1953 to 1966 the guillotine functioned twenty-two times; and each time the question of the death penalty arose, was debated in the public press, argued by intellectuals, by public officials, by the man in the street—and was dropped. According to Article 17 of the French Constitution, only the President of the Republic has the power over life and death, the power to commute the death sentence into one of life imprisonment.

In December of 1967 Gunther Volz was executed for rape and murder; during the Algerian war many were executed for assassination, for treason, and for other reasons involving the security of the state.

On March 12, 1969, Jean Olivier, convicted of having murdered two children aged ten and twelve years after raping one of them, was sent to the guillotine. Charles de Gaulle refused to commute his sentence. When Georges Pompidou took office that same year, he promised that while he occupied the position of President of the Republic, no one would be executed; and to prove his good faith, he swiftly commuted the three death sentences that had been handed down by the courts.

But in November of 1972, Monsieur Pompidou broke his promise. Once again the blade of the guillotine fell—upon the necks of Claude Buffet and of Roger Bontems, the first men to be executed in more than three years. Every newspaper in France plunged into the debate anew, for only one of the men had committed murder, yet both were sentenced to die. During a revolt at Clairvaux prison, Buffet had cut the throats of two prison officials who were held hostage, a man and a woman; Bontems had not killed, but he had done nothing to prevent the killings. Nonetheless President Pompidou withheld grace.

Over forty countries have abolished the death penalty, but according to a recent poll, the majority of French people are still in favor of capital punishment. And Georges Pompidou did not stay the guillotining of Ali

Benyares, a 34-year-old Tunisian convicted of killing a seven-year-old girl. At dawn on May 12, 1973, he stepped up to the scaffold, saying, "I ask France's pardon."

Monsieur de Paris still lives!

BIBLIOGRAPHY

ARCHIVES

Archives Nationales
Archives de la Seine
Archives du Cimetière de Montmartre
Archives, Musée de la Préfécture de Police
Archives, Paroisse de Saint Laurent

PERIODICALS

Le Moniteur Universel
Journal de France
Actes des Apôtres
Chronique de Paris
Journal de Perlet
Deux Amis
Le Thermomètre du Jour
Le Vieux Cordelier
Le Temps
Revue Retrospective
Le Figaro
Le Monde
Courier de France et de Brabant
Le Provincial
Le Vieux Saint-Maur
Mercure de France

Anecdotes du Temps de la Terreur—Paris 1856
Anecdotes sur les Décapités—Paris, An V de la République
Appert, Benjamin—Dix Ans à la Cour du Roi Louis Philippe—Paris
    1846
D'Avenal, Vicomte G.—Histoire Économique de la Propriété, des
    Salaires, des Denrées et de Tous les Prix en Général depuis
    l'An 1200 jusqu'en l'An 1800. 6 Volumes. Paris 1913
Balzac, Honoré de—Une Messe en 1793
Balzac, Honoré de—Un Episode sous la Terreur
Barbier—Chronique de la Régence ou Journal de Barbier, Avocat au
    Parlement de Paris—Paris 1728
Barras—Mémoires—Paris 1946
Beccaria—An Essay on Crimes and Punishments—1767
Bloehme—Notice sur la Guillotine—Paris 1865
Boustanquoi—Souvenirs d'Une Femme du Peuple
Bouteron, Marcel—Études Balzaciennes—Paris 1954

Brochard, Louis—Histoire de la Paroisse et de l'Eglise Saint-Laurent
à Paris. Paris 1923

Cabanes—Le Cabinet Secret de l'Histoire—Paris 1920

Cabanis, Georges—Sur le Supplice de la Guillotine—s.l.s.d.

Campardon, Émile—Marie Antoinette à la Conciergerie—Paris 1863

Camus, Albert—"Reflections on the Guillotine"—Evergreen Review
Reader, 1957–1967. Copyright 1957 by Grove Press, Inc.,
reprinted by permission of Calmann-Lévy, Editeur.

Carlyle, Thomas—The French Revolution

Casanova, Jacques de Seingalt—Mémoires, Écrits par lui-même.
Paris 1833–37

Castelot, André—Le Grand Siècle à Paris

Challamel, Augustin—Les Revenants de la Place de Grève—Paris
1897

Chereau, Achille—Guillotin et la Guillotine—Paris 1870

Christophe, Robert—Les Sanson, Bourreaux de Père en Fils pendant
Deux Siècles. Paris 1960

Cléry, Jean-Baptiste—Journal de Cléry pendant la Captivité de Louis
XVI—Paris 1906.

Collection Complète des Tableaux Historiques de la Révolution
Française Paris, An X de la République Française. 3 vols.

Cordier, l'Abbé Alphonse (De Tours)—Martyrs et Bourreaux de
1793. Paris 1856

Cottrell, Leonard—Madame Tussaud. London 1951

Créquy—Souvenirs de la Marquise de Créquy—1710–1802. Paris
1836. 6 vols.

Crocker, John Wilson—History of the Guillotine—London 1853

Dauban, C. A.—Les Prisons de Paris sous la Révolution, d'après les
Relations des Contemporains. Paris 1870

Dauban, C. A.—Paris en 1794 et en 1795, Composée d'après des
Documents Inédites. Paris 1869

Dornan, Paul—De Sanson à Deibler. Paris 1934

DuBois, Louis—Recherches Historiques et Physiologigues sur la
Guillotine. Paris 1843

Dumas, Alexandre—Le Drame de Quatre-Vingt Treize. Paris 1867

Durant, Will and Ariel—The Story of Civilization:
　The Age of Reason Begins
　The Age of Louis XIV
　The Age of Voltaire
　Rousseau and Revolution

Duval, G.—Souvenirs de la Terreur—Paris 1842

Elliott, Grace Dalrymple—Journal of my Life during the French
Revolution

Firmont, Abbé Edgeworth—Mémoires—Paris 1815

Firmont, Abbé Edgeworth—Letters to his Friends—London 1818

Fleischman, H.—La Guillotine en 1793—Paris 1908

Fleischman, H.—Anecdotes Secrètes de la Terreur—Paris 1908

Fornairon, Ernest—Fieschi, Le Chevalier Régicide

Fouquier, Armand—Les Causes Célèbres—Paris 1858–1867

Franklin, Alfred—Paris et les Parisiens au Seizième Siècle. Paris 1921

Funck-Brentano, F.—Les Brigands—Paris 1937

Funck-Brentano, F.—La Mort de la Reine

Garçon, Maurice—Histoire de la Justice—Paris s.d.

Gaxotte, Pierre—La Révolution Française—Paris 1962

Gaxotte, Pierre—Paris au XVIIIe Siècle—Paris 1968

Goncourt, Jules & Edmond de—La Societé Française pendant la
  Révolution. Paris 1889

Goulard, Roger—Une Lignée d'Exécuteurs des Jugements Criminels,
  Les Sansons. Melun 1968

Grison, Georges—Paris Horrible et Paris Original—Paris 1882

Hazen, Charles D.—The French Revolution—New York, 1932. 2
  vols.

Hebert—Mort de la Reine

Hillairet, J.—Connaissance du Vieux Paris—Paris 1954

Hillairet, J.—Promenades dans Paris—Paris 1936

Hillairet, J.—Gibets, Piloris et Cachots du Vieux Paris—Paris 1956

Hugo, Victor—Le Dernier Jour d'un condamné—Paris 18?

Hugo, Victor—Choses Vues—Paris 1913—Volume 1

Huysmans, J. K.—Là-Bas

Kershaw, A.—A History of the Guillotine—London 1958

Kroll, Maria—Letters from Liselotte, Elizabeth Charlotte, Princess
  Palatine and Duchess of Orleans. New York 1971 (Translated
  & Edited by Maria Kroll)

Lacroix, Paul—XVIIIe Siècle—Institutions, Usages et Costumes.
  Paris 1875

Lenôtre, G.—Le Tribunal Révolutionnaire—Paris 1908

Lenôtre, G.—La Guillotine et les Exécuteurs des Arrêts Criminels
  Pendant la Révolution—Paris 1903

Madelin, Louis—Figures of the Revolution—Paris 1929

Madelin, Louis—La Révolution—Paris 1938

Marquand, Henry E.—Ma Visite à Sanson, Bourreau de
  Paris—London 1865

Mémoire Pour les Exécuteurs des Jugements Criminels de Toutes les
  Villes du Royaume—Paris, Février 1790

Mémoires sur les Prisons

Mercier, L. Sebastien—Tableau de Paris—Paris 1780

Mercier, L. Sebastien—Paris pendant la Révolution, ou Le Nouveau
  Paris. Paris 1862—2 vols.

Michaud, L. G.—Biographie Universelle

Michelet, Jules—Histoire de la Révolution Française. Paris 1878

Montgaillard, G. H.—Histoire de France depuis la fin du Règne de
   Louis XVI—Paris 1827
Montesquieu, Charles Louis de Secondat—L'Ésprit des Lois
Moore, John—A Journal during a Residence in France. London 1794
   2 vols.
Morris, Gouverneur—Diary and Letters. New York 1888. Edited by
   Anne Cary Morris. 2 vols.
Mossiker, Frances—The Queen's Necklace—New York, 1961
Noailles, Marquise de—La Vie d'Anne-Paule-Dominique de Noailles
   Marquise de Montagu—Paris 1865
Pair, Georges—Messieurs Sanson, Bourreaux—Paris, 1938
Paris pendant La Terreur—Rapports des Agents Secrets du Ministre
   de L'Intérieur. Publiés par Pierre Caron. Paris 1910
Pichon, Ludovic—Code de la Guillotine—Paris 1910
Pottet, Eugène—Histoire de la Conciergerie du Palais de Paris. Paris
   1895
Quentin-Bauchart—Le Docteur Guillotin et la Guillotine. s.l.s.d.
Riouffe, H.—Mémoires d'Un Détenu. Limoges 1871
Robiquet, Jean—La Vie Quotidienne au Temps de la Révolution.
   Paris 1938
Roland, Madame—Mémoires Particuliers de Madame
   Roland—Paris 1855
Rousseau, Jean-Jacques—Le Contrat Social
Rousselet—Histoire de la Justice—Paris 1948
Rousselet—Les Souverains devant la Justice—Paris 1946
Saint-Edmé—Description Historique des Prisons de Paris—Paris
   1828
Saint Simon—Mémoires—Paris 1829
Sanson, Henri—Sept Generations d'Exécuteurs—1688–1847. Paris
   1862 6 vols.
Sanson—Mémoires pour servir à l'Histoire de la Révolution
   Française. Paris 1829 (Rédigés par Balzac et L'Héritier de
   L'Ain)
Sanson—Mémoires de l'Exécuteur des Hautes Oeuvres pour servir à
   L'Histoire de Paris pendant le Règne de la Terreur. Paris
   1830. Rédigés par A. Gregoire.
Sanson—Executioners All—Memoirs of the Sanson Family from
   Private Notes and Documents. 1688–1847. Edited by Henry
   Sanson, Late Executioner of the Court of Justice of Paris.
   London 1962
Savant, Jean—Le Vrai Vidocq—Paris 1957
Soubiran, André—Ce Bon Docteur Guillotin—Paris 1962
Stael-Holstein, Anne-Louise-Germaine—Considérations sur les
   Principaux Evenements de la Révolution Française. London
   1818 (Ouvrage posthume de Madame la Baronne de Stael)

Stendhal—Le Rouge et Le Noir

Stevenson, Gertrude Scott—The Letters of Madame. The Correspondence of Elizabeth Charlotte of Bavaria, Princess Palatine, Duchess of Orleans. New York 1925. 2 vols.

Surville, Mme. Laure (née de Balzac)—Balzac, Sa Vie et Ses Oeuvres d'après sa Corréspondance—Paris 1858

Thiers, Adolphe—Histoire de la Révolution Française—Paris 1853

Tussaud, John Theodore—The Romance of Madame Tussaud's. New York 1920

Tussaud, Marie—Madame Tussaud's Memoirs and Reminiscences of France. London 1838 (Edited by Francis Herve)

Turquan, Joseph—La Citoyenne Tallien. Paris s.d.

Vaissière, Pierre—Lettres d'Aristocrates—1789–94. Paris 1907

Vigée-Lebrun, Mme. Louise Elizabeth—Souvenirs. Paris 1835. 3 vols.

Voltaire—Le Siècle de Louis XIV—Paris 1818

Windtsor—Agonie et Mort Héroique de Louis XVI par le Citoyen Antoine, Vérité Windtsor—Paris, chez Cromwell au Palais de l'Égalité—1793

Zweig, Stefan—Marie Antoinette—New York, 1933

INDEX

[255]

[257]

[258]